HOME GROWN

In partnership with the

 Soil Association

HOME GROWN

A practical guide to self-sufficiency and living the good life

Foreword by Hugh Fearnley-Whittingstall

An Hachette Livre UK Company
www.hachettelivre.co.uk

First published in Great Britain in 2009 by Gaia,
a division of Octopus Publishing Group Limited
2–4 Heron Quays, London E14 4JP
www.octopusbooks.co.uk

ISBN: 978-185675-315-9

A CIP catalogue record for this book is available from the
British Library

Printed and bound in China

10 9 8 7 6 5 4 3 2 1

Produced and designed by: SP Creative Design
Wickham Skeith, Suffolk, England
Editor: Heather Thomas
Designer: Rolando Ugolini

Photography
Special photography by Rolando Ugolini
Additional photography by Charlie Colmer:
pages 110–111, 124, 129, 138, 170–171,
172, 176, 177, 182–183, 187, 191, 200
Soil Association photography courtesy of
www.soilassociation.org/images: pages 5, 9
(Rob Cousins), 10, 23, 24, 25, 74, 143, 153
Getty Images (Mel Yates) page 196, (Shaun Egars)
pages 196-197,(Buzz Bailey) page 197
Cover photograph: Pete Dodds

Acknowledgements
The publishers would like to thank the following
for their assistance in producing this book:
Johnny and Penny Marland

Contents

Contributors

Will Best

Will Best has been involved with livestock all his life. He grew up on a farm and has farmed organically in Dorset with his wife Pam for over 20 years. He converted his dairy farm to organics in 1988 and has since gone into partnership to form a company, Manor Farm Organic Milk Ltd, producing and marketing milk and cream throughout southern England.

Josephine Fairley

Josephine Fairley is a journalist and the author of a dozen books, including *The Ultimate Natural Beauty Book*. She has regular beauty updates on her website, www.beautybible.com. Josephine is also the co-founder of Green & Black's Organic Chocolate.

Penelope Hands

Penelope Hands is a writer, gardener and cook. She lives in an eighteenth-century house in Norfolk, England, with a large garden, where she grows many old varieties of apple and keeps bees and chickens.

Michael Michaud

Michael Michaud, together with his wife Joy, runs a boutique market garden specializing in chilli peppers. Michael was a domestic and international inspector for Soil Association Certification Ltd., as well as a programme evaluator for IFOAM (International Federation of Organic Agricultural Movements). He also served on the board of directors for the Soil Association and Soil Association Certication Ltd., and has worked on various committees for both organizations, including the Organic Seed and Soil Fertility Working Groups.

Francine Raymond

Francine Raymond has written several best-selling books on keeping hens and ducks, has has appeared on television and is a regular contributor to radio programmes, countless magazines and newspapers. She also runs workshops on poultry keeping at her home in Suffolk. Francine believes that raising hens naturally improves the ecosystem in the garden, allowing both birds and plants to produce to their full potential.

Judy Steele

Judy Steele has been an organic gardener for almost 30 years. She began her writing career at Farmers Weekly before turning freelance and focusing on organic issues. She wrote *Local Food Links: New Ways of Getting Organic Food from Farm to Table* for the Soil Association, was news editor of *New Farmer and Grower*, and has worked on an organic market garden. For several years, she edited *The Organic Way*, HDRA's quarterly magazine. She currently runs a Local Agenda 21 allotment project.

Elizabeth Winkler

Elizabeth Winkler is the editor of *Living Earth*, the Soil Association's membership magazine. She has written for *Parents* magazine, *Marie Claire*, the *Independent on Sunday* and the *Daily Mail*. An anti-GM campaigner, she had a political column 'Earthmother' in the *Bristol Evening Post*. She teaches journalism and is co-writing a novel.

Foreword

by Hugh Fearnley-Whittingstall

For most of us the phrase the 'good life' probably implies taking time out from the rat race, getting back to nature, 'growing your own' – and tucking in to some delicious home produce at the end of a hard day's digging. Of course this isn't practical for everyone. But some taste of the good life may be more practical than many of us might think.

It certainly helps to remember that we are all part of the same natural system as the animals, insects, plants and land that surrounds us. This can be hard, when we work long hours, eat industrially produced food and surround ourselves with manufactured goods. But in fact it is the food we eat that should serve as our daily reminder that, ultimately, we rely on the land and its produce to keep us healthy and happy.

Fortunately the Soil Association has recognized this for many years. Working to promote organic farming methods, it has been trying to foster the relationship between the health of the soil and that of plants, animals and people to help us create the kind of world most of us would prefer to live in. Organic farming ensures that animals are well cared for, plants are free from pesticides and that we show respect for our surroundings.

Part of the purpose of this book is to show you that everyone can share in the 'good life' by taking some small steps in the direction of self-sufficiency, and organic awareness. Whether it's starting to grow and eat your own vegetables, supporting local producers, or cleaning your loo with environmentally friendly products, there are things we can all do without too much effort. And for those wanting to make a bit more of a commitment, the possibilities are boundless, and hugely exciting. And so this book also reveals the practicalities and pleasures of keeping a few hens, a couple of goats or even a pair of pigs.

And pleasure is really the key. There's no enjoyment in tasteless fruit and vegetables sprayed with a cocktail of chemicals, meat from animals kept in misery, or products manufactured under appalling conditions. But as soon as you begin to free yourself from the ball and chain of dependence on industrially produced food, you enter a virtuous circle that is sure to change your life for the better. I'm constantly hearing from people who have just harvested their first veg, or gathered their first eggs, or are about to take the plunge with a pair of pigs. And without exception, they are loving it.

To some, the prospect of starting to raise your own food may seem difficult and daunting. Believe me, that's all psychological. You only have to take a few small steps to get started. For example, buy a few packets of seeds – choose vegetables you really like eating – and follow the instructions on the packet. Take a few tips from chapter 1 on looking after the soil, and you'll soon be cooking with the best vegetables you've ever had in your hands. And then you'll be ready for the next challenge.

Use this book project by project, year by year, and reclaim your right to a slice of the good life. You'll find it tastes delicious, and I reckon you'll keep coming back for more.

Hugh Fearnley-Whittingstall

Why eat home grown?

Eating home or locally grown produce means that you are living lightly – knowing that your lifestyle is replenishing the planet, not exhausting it. The Soil Association has been studying how to produce healthy crops and livestock without damage to the environment for over 50 years. Its philosophy and techniques are there to guide you as you begin your own personal journey towards sustainability. Whether you plan to grow your own organic vegetables, or buy them from your local farmers' market, this chapter shows you how living the good life is a win-win situation – you can care for yourself, your family, farm animals, wildlife and the environment, all in one.

A real solution

Agriculture is at the heart of society, and its effects, both good and bad, reach far and wide. The last 50 years of industrialized farming have led to environmental degradation and factory farming. Organic farming, by contrast, aims to farm with minimum harm to both farm animals and the countryside – it is the positive answer to problems caused by agrofarming.

In half a century, industrial agriculture has led to a system that exploits livestock, destroys wildlife and produces food that is soulless, and (remember BSE) sometimes even dangerous. In response, another way of farming has developed. The Soil Association, the world's first and oldest organic farming organization, has been working since 1946 to combine the best of traditional farming methods with the latest in ecological and agricultural science. Its underlying thinking is that a farm is not a production line, but a living system. Rather than dominating nature, the organic farmer aims to work with natural processes.

Healthy soil, healthy people

The Soil Association was founded by people who were concerned about the impact of intensive farming on the health of the soil, and its knock-on effect on health. In the following decades, as the organic pioneers predicted, the mineral levels in fruit and vegetables declined. According to government figures, between 1940 and 1991, mineral levels fell by up to 76 per cent. In contrast there is growing evidence that organic fruit and vegetables generally contain more nutrients than non-organic food. An independent review found that organic crops had significantly higher levels of 21 nutrients analyzed compared with non-organic produce.

Research also shows that organic crops tend to have more phytonutrients than non-organic crops. These naturally protect a plant against pests and disease (no need for pesticides) and are also thought to offer protection against cancer when the plants are eaten. Artificial fertilizers appear to increase the water content of a plant (hence a bigger yield), but the downside is a sappy plant with a diluted nutrient content. The Soil Association believes that more long-term research comparing organic with non-organic food is needed.

Organic farming protects the soil by:

- Restricting artificial chemicals because they suppress soil life
- Building fertility with crop rotation and by growing green manure
- Adding nutrients with compost and manure
- Encouraging smaller fields, windbreaks and hedgerows to reduce wind erosion
- Planting cover crops to protect the soil

The precautionary principle

This is a founding organic principle: if a significant risk exists, don't take it. The Soil Association sets organic standards based on the belief that any known toxin is a potential health hazard.

Organic farming seeks to farm without using chemical inputs. Organic standards ban all artificial fertilizers, herbicides, fungicides, and all pesticides bar seven – these can only be used as a last resort if organic methods have failed. And of those seven, five are severely restricted and all are under review. Compare this with over 430 pesticides that are allowed in non-organic agriculture, without any restrictions whatsoever.

The precautionary principle also applies to organic food after it is grown. Organic standards ban post-harvest chemical treatments, which are considered a health risk. As for food additives, health risks, including hydrogenated fats, monosodium glutamate and aspartame, are banned. The Soil Association permits only 30 of the most innocuous additives, mostly derived from natural sources, e.g. citric acid from lemon juice. Compare this to the 500 or so additives used without restriction by the non-organic food industry. Organic standards also ban all colourings (apart from anatto which is legally required in some cheeses), all artificial flavourings (30,000 are currently being used by the food industry), irradiation, and genetically modified organisms. Apart from in baby food, organic standards are the only regulations that restrict food additives.

Reducing cancer risks

Organic methods avoid pesticides which are potentially carcinogenic; pesticide residues are ranked among the top three environmental cancer risks by the US government. Is there a link between pesticides (UK agriculture uses 25,000 tonnes a year) and the increase in cancer rates? Sadly, instead of examining the possible links and preventing illness in the first place, most scientific research focuses on finding the 'magic bullet' that will cure cancer.

Positive health

Organic farmers believe that prevention is better than cure. Positive health helps avoid disease by giving a plant or animal the nutrients and care it needs to thrive – not drugs to cure illnesses that could have been prevented in the first place. And if disease appears, its role is to alert the attentive farmer that a problem needs addressing, not suppressing.

Positive health means an organic cow, suckled as long as possible as a calf, fed on a natural diet and housed with plenty of space. Less stressed, its immune system can cope with ill health. This applies to the web of life: a healthy soil produces healthy crops and healthy animals that eat them. Eating organic food helps people's positive health, too.

Good for animal welfare

Looking after animals the organic way is not only good for our health (if we eat dairy, meat or eggs) but can also make a dramatic difference to the lives of our farm animals. Organic standards, which are laid down in law, respect natural animal behaviour and ensure high standards of animal welfare.

The standards ensure that animals are truly free range, have plenty of space when housed and are fed an organic diet. The routine use of antibiotics is banned by the standards. Thanks to positive health, disease can be prevented before it can take hold. Compassion in World Farming says: 'Look for the Soil Association logo for a guarantee of the highest welfare standards in the UK'.

Good for wildlife

Industrialized farming can often result in monocultures where one crop is grown on large areas, year after year, creating larger fields which are dependent on artificial inputs. As a result, over the last 50 years in the United Kingdom, 95 per cent of our wildflower meadows have been lost, together with 50 per cent of woodland and 40 per cent of hedgerows. These were homes for plants and animals, and their destruction, coupled with the use of agrochemicals, which are designed to kill living things, has decimated wildlife. The decline of one species affects another, since they feed on one another. The result is that, in five decades, 82 per cent of partridges and 75 per cent of skylarks have vanished.

Organic farming can reverse this decline. Its farmers need insects and birds to eat pests. Its farming practice relies on an intact food chain, not on chemical pesticides. The last thing that organic farmers want to do is to kill the helpful predators, and thus they can conserve a bird's natural food.

Research shows that, when compared to non-organic farms, organic farms have 44 per cent more birds in the fields; more than five times as many wild plants in arable fields; and one-and-a-half times as many insects. Do you remember the vanishing skylarks? Research shows that more skylark chicks survive on organic farms because their insect food has not been wiped out by pesticides.

Good for the environment

Government studies show that organic farms are more energy efficient. They produce less of the greenhouse gas, carbon dioxide, than non-organic farms, as well as less dangerous waste. There is also lower pollution from sprays.

Initial research from the Rodale Institute, the organic research centre in the United States, suggests that organic farms can actively reduce carbon dioxide because of the organic soil's ability to 'lock up' carbon.

Organic standards

Organic farming is enforced by rules that are called organic standards. The Soil Association, which is the UK's largest and oldest organic certifier, is extremely experienced at ensuring that organic farms and businesses meet its rigorous standards for organic integrity.

The Soil Association strives to achieve the highest level of standards, not merely to meet the minimum legal requirements. The charity is especially well placed to better its standards because its certification 'arm' is not-for-profit. Rather than being driven by shareholders, it is governed by the Soil Association's philosophy of sustainability, as well as a general public with high expectations of its integrity.

Organic certification

The term 'organic' is a legal definition. It is the only food system (apart from baby food) that is inspected and certified under a rigorous annual inspection process. The Soil Association has been setting – and enforcing – standards longer than any other certifying body. The first product was certified in 1973, nearly two decades before the European Union produced its legislation. Therefore the Soil Association's know-how is unique – it is no wonder that it certifies over 70 per cent of the organic food that is sold in the UK.

Integrity

The Soil Association not only has experience; it also has integrity. Any surplus that is made by its not-for-profit certification 'arm' is ploughed straight back into the charity in order to raise awareness with the public, the media and policy makers about the benefits of growing and eating organic food.

The Soil Association has some of the highest organic standards in the world today, and its symbol, which is easily recognizable, is its guarantee to you that these high standards are being met.

Soil Association principles

Soil Association standards strive to meet fundamental principles that aim to:
- Coexist with, rather than dominate, natural systems.
- Sustain and/or build fertility.
- Minimize pollution and damage to the environment.
- Ensure the ethical treatment of animals.
- Protect and enhance the farm environment with particular regard to conservation and wildlife.
- Consider the wider ecological and social impact of agricultural systems.
- Maintain valuable existing landscape features and adequate habitats for the production of wildlife with particular regard to endangered species.

The organic movement

The Soil Association was founded in 1946 by people concerned about the industrialization of farming. They read the warning signs and understood the connections: an eroded soil depleted in nutrients leads to poor food quality and failing health. Using the best of the old and the new, they developed a way of farming that returns nature's goodness to the earth.

The organic movement sprang simultaneously from different quarters, as farmers, scientists, doctors and nutritionists all came to similar conclusions: that industrially-produced food was impoverishing the western diet. These far-sighted individuals saw how, following World War II, a system intended to produce cheap food could eventually damage the source of all food, the soil. They also analyzed the negative impact of chemical farming. For instance, the development of artificial fertilizers made animal manure, a natural soil fertilizer, redundant. Instead of mixed farms where livestock manure fed the soil and the soil produced healthy crops to feed the animals, both animals and crops became separated. This led to monocultures and factory farming, together with the needless suffering of animals, wildlife and the environment.

For the first 30 years of its existence, the Soil Association was involved mostly in research, building a body of knowledge about how to produce sufficient food with the least environmental impact. By combining the best of traditional farming methods with the very latest in modern techniques, the agriculture of the future was born.

Founding father

The agriculturist Sir Albert Howard was sent to India in 1905 by the British government to teach Indians how to farm, but he spent the next 35 years on research stations learning from Indian farmers. He discovered how an animal's healthy immune system can withstand disease, and how pests or disease are 'nature's professors' because they warn the farmer that something is wrong. He also understood the importance of compost to a healthy soil. 'The undernourishment of the soil is the root of it all,' he wrote.

Founding mother

Lady Eve Balfour learnt from Howard about the relationship between the health of the soil, and that of plants, animals and people. She was influenced by thinkers such as Sir Robert McCarrison who found that the Hunza people lived longer, healthier lives than their Western counterparts. Her book *The Living Soil* brought these ideas together, and led to the founding of the Soil Association in 1946. She allied practical farming experience with science and undertook research at her Suffolk farm, where the Soil Association was based for the first 30 years.

Nurturing the soil

Soil is wonderful because it provides the basic resources of our planet – life on earth depends on earth. Because the soil is so essential, organic farming has developed different techniques for looking after it. The main methods are composting and rotation, and these are simple techniques that you can use at home in your back garden.

Organic farming aims to work within a 'closed' system where as much as possible on the farm is recycled in order to build a nutrient-rich soil, rather than depending on artificial inputs from outside the farm.

Composting

Composting, the basis of organic farming, is recycling in action. To enrich the soil, the organic farmer will return unwanted plant material, together with waste produced by farm animals, back to the soil. Composting increases soil fertility, which, in turn, increases nutrients in the soil. So instead of being caught in a vicious cycle (see right), organic farming builds a virtuous cycle.

A fertile soil means one teeming with soil life: earthworms, beetles, centipedes, fungi, and bacteria so tiny that you need a microscope to see them (micro-organisms). They feed on waste, breaking it down into simpler and simpler forms of carbon until it becomes crumbly, nutrient-rich humus – the basis of soil.

Good composting both relies on a healthy soil life, and amplifies it. Research shows that organically managed soil that is enriched with compost and manure has more soil life (up to

85 per cent more) than soil which has been dosed with artificial fertilizers.

The non-organic farming industry assumes that plants can simply absorb artificial nutrients from the water in the soil. This kind of thinking does not take into account the complex role of soil life. Micro-organisms work on minerals, water and air to make the right conditions for plants to absorb nutrients. As a result, the more soil life there is, the more nutrients are retained in the soil.

Vicious cycles

There are two main types of agrochemicals: fertilizers to feed plants, and pesticides to control unwanted organisms. Both can lead to a chemical treadmill, where the use of one artificial input increases the use of another. Artificial fertilizers can degrade the soil, thus increasing the need for more artificial fertilizers to boost an ailing soil. Artificial fertilizers produce lush growth but, in turn, this attracts more pests, increasing the use of pesticides. In their turn, pesticides poison other living things other than the target pest, and they may also harm the soil life, which means that more artificial fertilizers are needed.

Rotation

Plants remove up to 60 minerals from the soil, and growing the same crops in the same soil every year can lead to a depletion of nutrients. Rotation is the heart of organic farming, ensuring that a crop that guzzles nutrients is followed the next year by one that replaces them.

An organic farmer's rotation includes growing green manure, like comfrey or clover, on up to a quarter of their land. Comfrey has deep roots which bring up minerals from lower soil levels; clover draws nitrogen from the atmosphere, so there is no need to add artificial nitrogen.

Green manures are incorporated into the soil and help recycle other nutrients, including phosphorus, potassium, calcium, magnesium and sulphur. Crop rotations also suppress pests, as well as weeds. The latest research shows that a green manure, such as rye,

exudes natural chemicals that will inhibit the germination of weed seeds for up to 30 days.

The problem with artificials

Factory-produced nitrogen can cause damage to the environment. In the first place, the manufacturing process uses a lot of oil, a non-renewable resource, and, when applied in the fields, it is easily washed away, causing pollution in rivers and streams. Non-organic farmers tend to replace the minerals used by plants with NPK fertilizers. These are based on

the theory that N (nitrogen), P (phosphorus) and K (potassium) are the only minerals a plant needs. This is not so. Organic farmers use compost and manures containing a wide variety of minerals that a plant needs, and not just NPK.

Genetic modification

The agrochemical companies are promoting genetic modification (GM) as the cure-all for farming problems which have been caused by agrochemicals in the first place. The Soil Association believes that GM has no place in farming. Firstly, the potential health effects of GM foods are unknown: there has been only one human feeding trial in the UK and this found that GM DNA transfers to human gut bacteria, a worrying effect that has not been followed up. Secondly, the environmental risks are irreversible and uncontrollable. In Canada,

one of the few places where GM crops are grown on a commercial basis, cross-pollination between GM and non-GM crops is already a reality. The result is a 'superweed', which is resistant to several herbicides and is hard to control. Another result is that organic crops are no longer organic. The province of Saskatchewan is unable to grow organic canola (oil seed rape).

To make matters worse, agrochemical companies are taking legal action against hundreds of North American farmers for growing GM crops without a licence – even when the GM seeds have arrived through accidental contamination. How will this affect the developing world? Forbidden to save GM seed, vulnerable to being sued and required to use only herbicides that work with herbicide-resistant GM crops, farmers will be even more trapped on the agrochemical treadmill.

It's not just about food

The more we understand about the pervasive effect of chemicals, the greater the demand for organic integrity in other areas of our lives apart from food. In response to this, the Soil Association has developed organic standards for textiles, and health and beauty products, too.

There is currently no legal framework governing non-food organic products, so there is no comeback for the consumer if a label claiming that a beauty product or T-shirt is organic turns out to be false. However, if a product bears the Soil Association symbol, you can be sure that its organic purity has been verified.

Organic cotton

Many people choose cotton because it is a natural fibre, but non-organic cotton is not exactly natural. Here are the facts: it takes about 30 teaspoons, or 150 grams, of chemicals to

grow the cotton for one T-shirt. The World Health Organization estimates that at least 20,000 people in developing countries, where most of the world's cotton is grown, die each year from pesticide poisoning. Non-organic cotton production uses large amounts of chemicals: a quarter of the world's insecticides are sprayed on non-organic cotton crops.

Fortunately, organic cotton can offer us an ethical, economically viable and environmentally sound alternative. It is reassuring to wear an organic cotton garment close to your skin, especially for people with allergies or babies with sensitive skin.

More than skin deep

It is estimated that our skin absorbs more than half of what we put on it. This is worrying when you consider that the majority of today's skincare products contain a cocktail of preservatives, petro-chemicals, preservatives and detergents. Many people turn to 'natural' cosmetics but what does that mean? The term 'natural' needs only one per cent of natural ingredients to qualify and can include up to 20 chemicals! However, a product bearing the Soil Association symbol means what it says: a product aiming to be as natural as possible.

What can you do?

If you want to create an organic lifestyle, just take one step at a time and do not expect the revolution to happen overnight. You can start by making everyday organic choices. You will find that as one decision leads to another, transformation will happen… organically.

Buy local

If you buy your organic produce at your local supermarket, think about buying it from your local farmer instead. There are many reasons why local food is the best choice. Seasonal local organic produce from your nearest farm means less packaging and fewer food miles: the distance food travels from source to plate. It also means less bargaining power for the big supermarket chains; more money for your local community (research shows that money spent locally doubles its value); more money for the grower selling direct; more affordability for you for the same reason (no middleman); and, last but not least, the produce is super fresh. You can support local organic farmers through organic box schemes, farmers' markets or buying direct from the farm.

Grow your own

This must be one of life's biggest satisfactions; not only does freshly-grown produce taste better, it is more economical, too. You do not need a large plot of land – even a small area of your garden can be prolific and supply many of your needs. If you want more space, consider applying for an allotment. Call your local council or the National Society of Allotment and Leisure Gardens for a fact sheet (see page 205). For more information on turning your back garden into an organic paradise, turn to page 206.

Compost kitchen waste

You can recycle waste and turn it into humus for your garden, whether you grow anything in your garden or not. Composting is a miracle, like turning base metal into gold. You can compost almost anything that has lived, but some things, like wood, take a long time to rot. Avoid meat and cooked food because they attract vermin. Also, too much citrus can make compost too acid. Most of your kitchen waste (tea bags, crushed eggshells, vegetable peelings) can alchemize into crumbly brown earth, rich in nutrients and soil life. All you need is a compost bin with a lid and a patch of ground to stand it on. Give it three to nine months. With the natural heat generated in the compost bin, what began looking like rubbish will become nutrient-rich humus, to be dug into your garden and enrich the soil.

A price worth paying

Research shows that the more people find out about the way food is produced, the more they choose organic food. High animal welfare, skilled husbandry, crop rotation and extra environmental measures result in organic food costing more to produce in the short term. Every time you spend a bit extra on organic food, you are voting with your purse for a more sustainable world. Keep the costs down by buying local and less processed organic foods. Keep some of your budget for organic cheese, meat or fish; you will feel good knowing the creatures were looked after well.

part 1

grow your own

Your soil

Before you can even start growing your own vegetables, herbs and fruit, you need to know that your soil is healthy and to analyze its properties and attributes. Is it sandy, clay or loam? Is it well drained or does it tend to hold water? Is it high or low in organic matter? All these considerations will affect which plants you decide to grow and how well they thrive. Healthy soil is not only the basis of successful organic gardening but is fundamental to life itself. By preparing and nurturing your soil and exercising some tender, loving care, you can grow healthier crops which may be higher in nutrients.

Soil profiling

Soils are naturally divided into layers, or horizons. Digging a pit into the soil produces a profile that reveals these different horizons. Profiling has practical applications, enabling you to uncover potential drainage problems and also to devise cropping and tillage strategies.

The upper layer of soil is the topsoil, and this is the substance that is most often associated with the word 'soil'. It is generally darker in colour due to the accumulation of organic matter. Most of the soil's organisms and much of its fertility are here, too.

Just below the topsoil is the lighter-coloured and less fertile layer of the subsoil. The depths of these two horizons will vary, and any cultivation must be done in such a way that they are not mixed together.

If you dig down even deeper in the pit, you will come to a third horizon, which consists of the parent material from which the topsoil and the subsoil originated. Digging a pit can also reveal the presence or absence of a hard pan – a distinct layer of compacted soil that prevents root penetration and downward movement of water.

Life forms

The soil is a thriving menagerie of life forms from both the plant and animal kingdoms. They include the more obvious plant roots and moles, as well as snails, slugs and insects. There are also the microscopic organisms, such as fungi, nematodes and bacteria, which are unseen but no less significant in the roles they play.

The organisms residing in a soil will affect its physical and chemical properties as well as influencing the health and productivity of the crops growing in it. The do-gooders decompose organic matter and extract gaseous nitrogen from the air, while there are also pathogens that can infect plants and ruin their health if the soil's balance is not right. Earthworms make their presence known by burrowing through the soil and improving its drainage, structure and fertility. Like any other community, the soil is a mix of the predatory and benign, all contributing to the make-up of an ever-changing ecosystem.

What is soil?

Soil is a synergistic amalgamation of different parts. Giving it form is a framework of mineral matter ranging in size from large boulders down to fine clays. Pores take their place among the mineral parts, giving air and water a place to reside. All manner of plant and animal life contribute to a soil. Added to this mix is organic matter in varying states of decay. When the mineral nutrients are finally factored in, the results are soils with the potential to support the long-term production of healthy and health-giving crops.

Living space

Pores make up between 40 and 60 per cent of the volume of a soil. They are filled with water and air, with the proportions of each affected by the amounts added by rainfall and irrigation; the volume taken up by plants through their roots; and the quantities lost by evaporation from the surface. The pores vary in size from small to large, and good soil management encourages a balance between air-filled pores and a crop's need for water.

Solid as a stone

The solid part of most soils is dominated by mineral matter which comes in a range of sizes. Some of the larger material (flint, stones and gravel) can interfere with cultivation and seed sowing while wearing down plough shares, rotavators' tines and tyres. Small amounts can be tolerated but avoid soils crammed full of these large pieces of mineral, especially where annual crops are grown.

The smallest-sized minerals in soils are particles of sand, silt and clay. Sand particles are the largest, and can be anywhere from 0.06 mm to 2 mm in diameter, while clays, the smallest, are less than 0.002 mm in diameter. Silts, of course, fall in between. Soils usually contain a mix of all three particles, and the relative quantities of each determine a soil's 'texture', chemical properties and physical attributes. Texture can be determined by the 'feel' method – knead a sample of wet soil between the fingers and thumb. This little test will help to tell you whether the soil is sandy (gritty), clay (sticky) or silt (silky and soapy).

Sandy soils

These feel gritty and fall apart when rolled into a ball. They are dominated by large pores, are free-draining and need frequent watering during a drought. They also tend to be low in fertility since their nutrients leach out with excess rain or irrigation water. On the plus side, sandy soils warm up quickly in the spring, are easy to cultivate and can be worked soon after wet weather. They are good for growing long-rooted vegetables, like parsnips and carrots.

Clay soils

These are sticky and can be rolled into a sausage shape. Their pores are small and slow to drain. They leach fewer nutrients than sandy soils, and their fertility and organic matter levels are higher. When they dry out, they tend to turn hard and are difficult to dig. They are slow to heat up in the spring, especially if wet.

Silt soils

These are not very sticky or gritty, and have a buttery, silky or soapy feel, like talcum powder. They are less water retentive than clay, but are slower draining than sand. Their nutrients are also less prone to leaching than a sandy soil.

Loams

These are a mixture of sand, silt and clay in proportions that give each type of particle equal control over the soil's chemical and physical properties. The best agriculture soils are loams. If well managed, they are easily worked, like sands, but with the moisture retention and nutrient levels of silts and clays.

Sound structure

The particles of sand, silt and clay in a soil do not act individually but are stuck together into 'aggregates'. This is called 'structure' and occurs throughout the soil profile. Water movement, aeration and porosity are influenced by structure, affecting the speed at which soils heat up in spring; the extent of root growth; and the biological activity of the resident life.

Good soil management will encourage a stable granular or crumb structure in the topsoil. This will produce the fine tilth which is needed by germinating seeds and growing plants. This is promoted by digging in bulky, organic matter; by keeping tillage operations to an absolute minimum; and by including some fibrous-rooted green manures in your cropping programme.

Wet soil

The structure will be weak when soils are wet, so cultivations must be carried out only when the conditions are dry enough to prevent any damage to the aggregates. Improving the drainage of water-logged soils will also help (see page 34). Since wet aggregates are easy to crush, vegetable growers should try using a bed system in order to limit the foot and tractor traffic to any paths that border the growing areas (see page 55).

Similarly, grazing animals should be taken off pastures during the wet winter months to prevent any trampling damage to the point where the soil's aeration and water drainage are adversely affected.

Silt and sandy soils

Light-textured silt and fine sandy soils, which are low in organic matter, will have poor structural stability. When they are pounded by heavy rains or irrigation, their aggregates break down and form hard crusts, or caps, which restrict seedling emergence. Soils that are prone to capping should not be watered after sowing, but if it is absolutely necessary, then the water should be applied frequently and gently as fine drops.

Organic matters

Besides pore space and mineral matter, soils will contain organic matter in varying degrees. Peaty soils, for example, can have over 25 per cent organic matter, although the norm in the topsoil is between one and six per cent, and in the subsoil it is usually less than two per cent.

The organic matter is actually made up of dead and decaying plants and animals which are broken down gradually into humus, which is a chemically-complex, dark-coloured and rather stable substance, which is synthesized by microbes.

Organic matter has an influence far beyond the modest proportions that are found in soils, and its importance cannot be overstressed. For example, it provides mineral nutrients to plants and is a food source for soil organisms. It also improves soil structure and it may help to control plant diseases. Because of its chemical make-up, organic matter protects valuable nutrients from leaching out in rain water, thereby indirectly influencing soil fertility.

Adding organic matter

If you have a clay soil, then the addition of plenty of organic matter will make it not only easier to work but it will also be better drained and aerated. The water-holding capacity of sandy soils will also be increased by such treatments. In addition, some organic matter which is applied as a mulch will help to prevent water loss and reduce soil erosion.

Loss of organic matter

The loss of organic matter from the soil is a natural phenomenon which is accelerated by high temperatures, improved aeration and liming. You will find that soils need to be topped up constantly in order to sustain their levels. Fortunately, this happens naturally in an organic system, where green manuring and the addition of bulky organic materials is a normal practice.

Litmus test

The acidity and alkalinity of a soil are always measured in pH units that range on a scale from 0 to 14. The majority of soils are in the pH range of 4.5 to 7.5 although some chalky or calcareous soils can reach 8.0 to 9.0.
- Neutral soils have a pH 7.0.
- Alkaline soils are over 7.0.
- Acid soils fall below 7.0.

Matching soil and crop pH

The pH affects the nutrient availability and biological activity in the soil. Bacteria are less active and molybdenum is less available in acidic soils; manganese and iron deficiencies occur at high pH values. A low pH inhibits potato scab, while a pH of 7.0 or above keeps brassica clubroot in check. Some crops, such as blueberries, thrive in acid soils whereas others, like lucerne, prefer more alkaline ones. Good husbandry means matching up the soil pH and the pH requirements of the crop.

Adjustment tests

Except for chalky or calcareous soils, the natural tendency is for soils to become more acid. There are some simple-to-use proprietary tests that can be used to determine whether a pH adjustment is needed. If this is the case, you should apply limestone, made primarily of calcium carbonate, to neutralize the acidity. Alternatively, dolomite or dolomitic limestone, which is mostly calcium-magnesium carbonate, performs much the same function, although it can supply magnesium, too.

Down the drain

Good drainage is a sign of a healthy soil. It means that plant roots are well-aerated and that they are getting the oxygen they need to support strong, vigorously-growing plants.

Improving drainage

Poorly-drained soils can become water logged and must be improved to make them more amenable to growing crops. If a soil has a hard pan holding up water, then the drainage can be improved by breaking up the pan through a process of either deep digging or subsoiling. Sometimes a clay subsoil hinders water movement, and working some organic matter into the clay may open it up.

Raised beds and a stable granular structure in the topsoil will also help to improve the drainage. If all else fails, a drainage system made of rubble-filled trenches or some special drain pipe can be put in.

Coping with erosion

Soil erosion is destructive and non-sustainable, allowing the top soil, along with its organic matter, fertility and life, to be washed away and lost. It starts when raindrops striking the soil detach particles from the surface, and continues as water moving over the soil carries these particles along with it. Erosion is a problem on sloping land, and the longer and steeper the slope, the more likely it is to occur. There are effective control measures.

- Mulch with bulky organic matter to lessen the impact of raindrops and to slow any water running down the slope.
- Promote a stable granular structure to improve water infiltration into the topsoil and reduce the amount of surface run-off.
- Use steeply sloping land for permanent pasture and grazing.
- Plant slightly sloping fields with annual crops if they go along the contour rather than up and down the incline.

Caring for your soil

Healthy soils grow productive crops. However, these soils do not happen magically; they are created by attentive gardeners and farmers who know and respect their role in the food-growing chain.

Fertility

Plants require at least 16 nutrient elements for growth. These include carbon, hydrogen and oxygen, which are utilized from air and water and make up most of the plant tissue. They also need macronutrients – nitrogen, calcium, phosphorous, potassium, magnesium and sulphur – in relatively large quantities; as well as micronutrients – boron, zinc, molybdenum, manganese, iron, copper and chlorine.

Boosting the soil's fertility

Macro- and micro-nutrients are absorbed from the soil, although they are not always present in large enough quantities to satisfy a crop's requirements. The fertility levels, therefore, must be boosted to help crop production along, and you can employ different strategies for this. The use of highly soluble fertilizers, both man-made and natural, is prohibited or restricted by organic standards. In general, if you are planning to improve the fertility of your soil, you should give priority to recycling nutrients within your garden or smallholding, while reducing the need for brought-in materials.

Low density

Bulky organic materials can be used either as mulches (see page 53) or worked into soils to increase their levels of organic matter (see page 33). They also play a valuable role in supplying plant nutrients, although their concentrations vary widely. Peat, for example, is low in nutrients and is almost useless as a nutrient source. Similarly, fibrous materials, such as sawdust, should be approached with caution, since they use nitrogen from the soil as they decompose, thereby depleting the amount available for plants. Garden composts and animal manures are in a different class and, when they are compared to other bulky materials, they are nutrient rich. Nevertheless, they are still a poor source of fertility in comparison to more concentrated fertilizers, and need to be used in large amounts to supply a crop's nutrient needs.

Animal manures

Animal manures are made up of faeces and urine (except for poultry manure, which has no urine), plus the straw or other material used as bedding. The nutrient value of manure varies widely, and it will depend on the animal species from which it comes; the type and quantity of bedding material used; and the handling and storage conditions.

In the spirit of sustainability, home-produced manures are the first choice for organic production systems. For gardeners and smallholders with no animals, the next-best things are manures sourced from a local organic farm with livestock.

Of course, there are also manures from non-organic farms where exported nutrients can easily be replaced by bagged fertilizers. However, non-organic manures reflect modern agricultural practices and, therefore, should be used only after a careful investigation. The animals they come from, for example, should not be given feeds with GM ingredients. There are also ethical considerations, especially with manures from intensively-raised chickens and pigs. Horse manures, too, present a problem since they may come laden with persistent wormers that take a while to break down.

Garden composting

Composting is a decomposition process that reduces plant and animal by-products to a dark, crumbly material. It recycles kitchen, garden and animal wastes, reducing the need for importing soil improvers and fertility. Without some form of composting, a garden or smallholding cannot be organic.

Successful composting establishes a moist and well-aerated environment in which bacteria, fungi and other organisms can thrive. Wet and soft green material, which is high in nitrogen (including raw kitchen wastes, fresh plants and grass clippings), should be mixed with dry material, which is high in carbon (such as dead leaves and straw). With the right combination of ingredients, composting will start spontaneously without the need for further encouragement.

Applying animal manures

Whatever their source, animal manures must be managed in ways that make the full use of their potential.
- Whether organic or not, they should be applied only after they have been properly composted or well-rotted.
- Nutrients are highly soluble so you should prevent losses through leaching by covering heaps that are stacked outdoors with plastic or another inert, impermeable material.
- Manures from chickens are especially rich in nitrogen, and therefore should be mixed with straw and used more sparingly than those from sheep, cattle and horses.

Not everything, unfortunately, can be composted. Meat and fish, dog and cat faeces, and coal ash, for example, should be left out. Disposable nappies are also a no-go area. Perennial weeds can go in, but only after they have died off – otherwise they may start growing in the compost heap.

Hot composting

When it comes to composting, there are enough tried-and-true techniques to keep even the most demanding gardener happy. Gardeners needing a quick fix of compost can try hot composting. The waste materials are composted at one go, initially heating up to temperatures that are hot to the touch before eventually cooling down. The material should be turned to generate more heat and hurry the process along. Most weed seeds and diseases are killed by the high temperatures generated during the process, though material infected with persistent diseases, such as onion white rot, may survive and thus should be excluded from the compost.

Cold composting

This is a protracted affair that can take more than a year to complete. Wastes are added to the pile as they become available, making it a practical approach when there is not enough material to compost at one time. Cold composts may or may not heat up, and, because of this uncertainty, there is no way of knowing if any disease organisms, brought in on garden plants, have been killed. Weed seeds, too, may survive the composting process, so only seedless weeds should be added.

Worm composting

This method uses tiger worms, which are found naturally in compost and manure heaps. Collected from existing heaps, the worms are then confined to containers that provide them with a cool, moist environment. Commercially-made plastic wormeries are available but are quite expensive. If you are frugal by nature and reluctant to spend your hard-earned cash, something as simple as a wooden box will do. The worms will thrive on a varied diet that includes vegetable peelings, annual weeds and even paper. Although they are not overly fussy about what they eat, they are modest eaters and need only a little food at a time.

Liquid feeds

Liquid feeds are used to boost the growth of transplants, pot-grown plants and nutrient-stressed plants which are already established in the garden. Although proprietary materials are readily available in garden centres and catalogues, DIY versions are easy to make. All that is needed is a large tea bag made from a porous material, such as jute. Fill the bag either with some manure, comfrey leaves or wild nettles, and then steep it in a barrel of water or other large container.

Comfrey is a particular favourite, probably because it is so undemanding a crop to grow. Plants can last for years, and they are a doddle to propagate from offsets or cuttings taken from the roots. Comfrey, however, is like a bad reputation – easy to get but hard to get rid of – and the patch where it grows should be permanently abandoned to its cultivation.

Green manuring

Green manures are plants that are cultivated specifically for improving the soil. As they grow, they smother weeds, protect the soil structure from the ravaging effects of rain, and sop up nutrients that would otherwise be leached out. Fibrous-rooted crops, such as grazing rye and ryegrass, can promote soil structure, while legumes, such as clovers, contribute much-needed nitrogen. Green manures are eventually worked into the soil where they decay and add to the pool of nutrients and organic matter already there.

Not all is good news with green manures, and crops recently incorporated into the soil will physically interfere with the preparation of the fine seedbed that is needed for seed sowing and germination. In addition to this physical meddling, green manure residues can also release chemicals that inhibit seed germination. Both problems can be overcome by waiting. In a vegetable plot, however, the wait can be shortened if transplants are used. They are better adapted to coarsely-prepared soils and less susceptible to the toxic substances given off by the decomposing green manures.

Legume green manures

These are members of the *Fabaceae* family and include lucerne, clover and vetch. Shortly after germination, they establish a symbiotic relationship with *Rhizobium* bacteria, which take up residence in the nodules formed on the roots. The legumes contribute high-energy carbohydrates to the bacteria, which reciprocate the favour by passing on the nitrogen that they have extracted from the air. This nitrogen is used by the legumes for their own growth and is available to other plants when the legumes decompose in the soil.

There are different species of *Rhizobium* bacteria, and a given species will associate with some legumes but not with others. For example, the *Rhizobium* of red and white clovers are naturally found in British soils, and the symbiotic partnership between plant and bacteria is easily established. However, these same bacteria will not associate with fenugreek and lucerne, and therefore another species of the bacteria must be brought in as a commercially-produced culture or nitrogen fixation is unlikely to occur.

Non-legume green manures

These include ryegrass, grazing rye, phacelia and mustard, and they form no relationships with *Rhizobium* bacteria. This does not, however, make them any less valuable, and they have a role to play in well-designed rotations. Exercise caution, however, with brassicas like mustard: they should not be grown where club root is a problem.

Annual green manures

These include grazing rye and winter tares and are for short-term use only. Cut when they are still young, they can be either incorporated into the soil or left as a mulch on the surface.

Longer-duration green manures

Holdings of one or two hectares may benefit from these manures, which are recruited from perennial plants used for pastures. Good for a year and more, they can be grown alone, as in the case of red clover or lucerne, or used in various mixes of legumes and grasses, such as ryegrass, timothy, and red and white clovers. They are also flexible in their management requirements and can be cut and left in situ; made into hay; or grazed by livestock. When their time comes, work them into the soil so the next crop can benefit from their goodness.

Rotation

This is a system of production that avoids year-after-year cropping of related plants on the same piece of ground. It effectively controls the build-up of pests and diseases and is at the core of organic farming and growing.

Rotations are usually based round plant families (see page 59) with Soil Association Standards prohibiting outdoor crops of potatoes and the *Alliaceae* and *Brassicaceae* families 'returning to the same land before a period of three seasons has elapsed'. Continuous cropping of alliums, brassicas and potatoes in greenhouses and tunnels is also prohibited. The prohibitions may not go far enough and probably should include other crops and families too. Similarly, the breaks could be longer and the standards recommend that 'rotation should be planned to allow the longest period possible between growing crops of the same family'.

Properly designed rotations

Rotations are not just about controlling pests and diseases. If designed properly, they should include legumes to fix nitrogen, fibrous-rooted crops to improve soil structure, and green manure crops to increase organic matter levels. Leafy crops, like brassicas and potatoes, compete well with annual weeds and may be grown to clean up the ground for subsequent, less competitive crops, such as carrots and onions. A good example of rotation would be two years of grass and clover followed by potatoes, cabbage and then carrots. A green manure, such as vetch, should be planted after autumn harvesting to protect the soil over winter. This should be turned in in spring prior to planting the subsequent crop. There is no definitive rotation that suits all gardens and smallholdings. The best we can do is to follow the principles, observe the results and adjust the cropping patterns as necessary.

Vegetables and herbs

Growing your own vegetables and herbs is one of the easiest ways of making a firm commitment to going organic. It's fun to do and you will be able to enjoy experimenting with a whole range of unusual varieties that are not available on the supermarket shelves. Nothing ever tastes as good or as fresh as vegetables that you have tended lovingly and grown yourself. You don't need a huge garden for growing vegetables and herbs – even a relatively small plot can produce quite high yields and will provide for some of your culinary needs.

The groundwork

Before any sowing and planting can be done, the soil must be worked into a condition that will promote seed germination and support crop growth. At the same time, the groundwork can be used to bury weeds and green manures, mix in lime and fertilizers and incorporate animal manures and composts. Cultivations should be kept to a minimum at all times, and must be done only when soil conditions are right.

Soil preparation is typically done in two steps:
- The first loosens the soil.
- The second smooths out the surface and creates a tilth for sowing and transplanting.

Loosening the soil

In small gardens, digging is the best way to loosen the soil for growing vegetables. You can do it in a reasonable amount of time without taxing your enthusiasm. In its simplest form, digging is restricted to turning over the topsoil with either a fork or a spade. It is normally done to a depth of 25 cm (10 in) – about the blade length of a spade – although this would be less where the topsoil is thin.

Double working

If you want to work the soil to greater depths, then you need to use a more complicated two-staged operation. First remove the topsoil to a depth of 25 cm (10 in) – less in gardens with thinner topsoils – and then loosen the exposed soil underneath with a fork before covering it over with the topsoil.

Despite the extra digging and hard work involved, this double working is an effective antidote to hard pans and compaction. It will give the crop roots more depth from which to extract water and nutrients from the soil.

Using machinery

If you have a large garden, then you may need to use a machine, such as a tractor-mounted plough, to turn over the upper layer of soil. Since ploughing is ineffective against deep-lying hard pans, use a subsoiler to loosen up the soil below the ploughed layer.

Smoothing things out

The second step in groundwork breaks up clods of soil, smooths out the surface and produces a fine-structured tilth. If you have a small garden, then you need nothing more than a rake to do the job, but if you have a large garden, then you may require tractor-mounted cultivators and harrows.

Rotavators can also be a useful tool since they both loosen the soil and produce a fine tilth in the upper layers. They must, however, be used judiciously since over-cultivation can lead to a breakdown of soil structure and the formation of pans.

Starting from seed

Contrary to their inert look, seeds are living organisms that exist in a dehydrated state of suspended animation. Each one has an embryo and enough stored food to get it through germination – all it needs is enough air, sufficient water and the right temperature to germinate.

Getting things started

Ideally, seeds should be sown in a moist, well-structured soil or propagating compost made up of fine particles. When soil or compost is packed down firmly over the seeds, they take in water and swell up. Using the stored food, the embryos then develop roots, which stretch downwards, and shoots, which push upwards to the surface. By the time the shoots emerge, the seeds have evolved into seedlings that are ready to grow on their own.

Buried alive

If seed is sown too deeply, then the seedlings will run out of food before they even surface and therefore they will suffer an untimely subterranean death. Because large seeds have more food reserves than small ones, they can be sown deeper in the soil or compost. Thus, as a comparison, the large seeds of beans can go down 50 mm (2 in) deep, whereas the more diminutive carrot and lettuce seeds are unable to survive depths of more than 20 mm (3/4 in).

Putting on the heat

Different crops respond differently to their surroundings, and each one has an optimum temperature range for germination. Thus onions and leeks are at their best from 7–21°C (45–70°F), whereas cabbages, peas and broad beans will peak at between 6°C (43°F) and a remarkable 32°C (90°F).

Sensitivity to low temperatures

Some crops are especially sensitive to low temperatures, and these will need extra warmth for successful germination. Tomatoes and sweet corn, for example, will require temperatures that are above 10–12°C (50–54°F). However, despite their high standards, they are not as demanding as peppers, which will need temperatures of 15°C (59°F) and above.

Monitoring the soil temperature

Seeds that are sown when temperatures are too cold may rot. To avoid any crop failures, sowing should be done only when the soil or the compost is warm enough to stimulate germination. Temperatures can be monitored with a soil thermometer, taking some of the guesswork out of sowing.

Numbers game

A garden's success will depend on you sowing seeds that are able to produce uniform stands

of healthy plants. Only the best-quality seeds will deliver this goal, and therefore it is always a false economy to buy anything second-rate, no matter how attractive the price.

Increasing life expectancy

Like all living things, seeds are not immortal. As soon as they are harvested, they start to deteriorate, eventually dying if they are kept long enough. Heat and humidity will hasten their demise, whereas cool, dry surroundings will increase their life expectancy.

To create these optimum conditions and prevent premature deterioration, all you will need is a plastic food storage box or similar airtight container. Just pack the seeds into the container with some silica gel (this is available from most photography shops and chemists), then seal it and store in a place where the year-round temperature is 10°C (50°F) or less – the best option is probably the refrigerator.

Direct seeding

Crops are, more often than not, established from seed that is sown directly into their final growing places. This 'direct seeding' method means that after the seeds germinate, the seedlings are left to mature where they are.

Methods of direct seeding

There are several ways in which you can go about direct seeding, as described below:
• Narrow troughs called 'drills' can be drawn in the soil, and a single line of seeds dropped into each one.

• If wider troughs are made in the soil, then the seeds of closely-spaced crops, such as coriander and radish, can be spread evenly as bands in the bottoms of the drills.
• Alternatively, large-seeded vegetables, such as peas and sweet corn, can be sown singly into holes that are poked in the ground.

Transplants from seeds

Transplanting is the practice of moving plants from one place to another. In the case of crops grown from seed, the seeds are sown in one place, where they germinate and produce seedlings. When the seedlings are big enough to move, they are planted elsewhere to mature. This method has several advantages over direct seeding, as well as giving you flexibility and a new dimension to gardening.

Along with its benefits, transplanting also has its limits. It may, for example, be too labour-intensive to transplant closely-spaced crops, such as coriander, while the long-rooted carrots and parsnips tend to fork if they are transplanted.

Ready-grown transplants can be bought from garden centres and nurseries, but if you are striving for self-sufficiency, you may prefer to grow your own. A number of techniques have been devised over the years.

Compost-based methods

One method of transplant production is based on the use of bought-in propagating composts which encourage seed germination and seedling growth. Not to be confused with garden compost, the composts used for propagation are spiked with nutrients and adjusted to the correct pH, while being well-structured, well-aerated and well-drained. They should also be free from pests, diseases and weed seeds, although weeds particularly can sometimes be a problem.

The most popular brands of propagating composts for vegetable gardening are made either from peat or coir fibre, which is taken from coconut husks. Both of these, however, come burdened with issues of sustainability (the peat is mined from bogs, while the coir fibre is shipped from India and Sri Lanka), and more environmentally-concerned gardeners should look for sustainable alternatives.

One possibility is composted green waste which is produced specifically for propagation. There are some 'organic' makes on the market (presumably using acceptable fertilizers while being free from GM materials), but they should be tested before being adopted on a large scale.

Ambitious gardeners with small vegetable plots can try making their own propagating composts from ingredients such as worm compost, leaf mould and comfrey. Innovative individuals and gardening organizations have devised their own recipes; try these before making up something new.

Module living

A relatively new method of transplant production uses specially-designed seed trays called modules. These are divided into individual cells which are filled with compost. You sow the seeds into the cells, then keep the trays either in a heated propagator or an unheated structure, such as a greenhouse. The final site will depend on the crop, the time of year and your own personal whims.

The normal goal is to grow only one seedling per cell. However, some crops can be multi-seeded and grown at higher populations of plants in each cell. The extent of the population increase depends on the crop, and varies from three to four seedlings per cell for turnips, four to five for bulbing onions, and seven to eight for salad onions. The seedlings are transplanted as a group, though the distance between the groups is greater than for single plants.

Once the roots fill the cells, take the seedlings with their compost out of the trays and relocate them in the garden soil. Crops destined for tunnels or greenhouses can go directly to their final resting place. Those going outside, however, should be kept in their trays and moved to the cooler outdoors to be hardened off before transplanting. This will toughen up the seedlings and prepare them for a less pampered life in the open air.

Benefits of seed-grown transplants

- Getting a jump on pests and weeds.
- Coddling small and expensive seeds that might otherwise get lost in the garden soil.
- Timely sowing of outdoor crops in wet springs.
- Getting a head start on warm season crops like tomatoes and cucumbers.

Seed trays and pots

Warm season crops, like peppers, tomatoes and aubergines, will respond to heat at every stage of their growth. Starting in February or March, scatter their seeds into compost-filled trays and put them into heated propagators to stimulate germination.

After the seeds germinate, gently tease the seedlings out of the trays – in a time-honoured practice called 'pricking out' – and transplant into plastic pots filled with compost. The heating should be continued, and the pots either kept in the propagator or moved into a mini-tent constructed inside a tunnel or a greenhouse. A mini-tent is inexpensive to make from plastic sheets or film, and it can be fitted out with a heater which you should turn on when the temperature drops. Because it is small, a tent like this is quite cheap to heat.

Around April or May, when the pots have been infiltrated with enough roots to hold the compost together, the young plants can be transplanted to the greenhouse or tunnel soil. With warmth and sunshine, harvesting should begin some time in July or August.

Bare-rooted transplants

With bare-rooted transplanting, seeds are sown directly into the garden soil – either outdoors or under cover – where the seedlings grow until they are lifted and transplanted elsewhere. Unlike compost-based propagation, this technique has the advantage of requiring no special equipment, although the seedlings have to put up with competition from weeds and the unwanted attention of slugs at all stages of their development.

Growing bare-rooted transplants is generally restricted to leeks and brassicas, such as kale, sprouts and cabbage. The seedlings are closely spaced in rows, about 25 cm (10 in) apart, and are ready for transplanting when the brassicas are about 15 cm (6 in) tall and the leeks as thick as a pencil. After watering the day before, you should loosen the soil with a fork – the seedlings are gently pried out of the ground with as little damage to the roots as possible.

Handling transplants

Transplanting seedlings can be done either by hand or by using a transplanting machine which is pulled behind a tractor. Whichever method you choose to use, the move from one site to another traumatizes the seedlings, damaging their roots and checking their growth. However, their re-establishment can be facilitated by transplanting them into a well-worked soil on a dull day. You should follow this up with some frequent light waterings in order to keep the soil around the roots moist.

Bed time

One of the best ways of growing vegetables and herbs is in a bed system whereby the crops are laid out in squares and rectangles. Foot traffic and tractors must be confined to pathways between the beds in order to reduce any compaction on the beds themselves.

If you have a large garden or smallholding, you may use a tractor for sowing, transplanting and weeding crops. In small gardens, the beds must be narrow enough so that their centres are only an arm's length away, allowing the middles to be reached from the paths.

Beds can be either flat or raised. You can build up raised beds using the topsoil in the paths. They can improve drainage of heavy soils, especially during winter in high rainfall areas. They often succumb to rainfall erosion, but can be made more permanent if they are enclosed inside wooden, plastic or brick edging.

No-dig gardening

Practitioners of no-dig gardening forgo the tradition of turning the soil, preferring instead to mulch the surface with organic matter. Earthworms that thrive under the mulch replace the work done by spades and forks, hauling the organic matter into their tunnels and improving the soil's fertility and structure (see page 35).

However, you cannot abandon your gardening tools completely, and some soil disturbance is inevitable. For example, you will need to dig some holes for transplanting, and you may need to prise root crops out of the ground with a fork. Compacted soils may also need to be loosened up before the no-dig technique is adopted. Although the perfect no-dig garden may not be possible, soil tillage can still be reduced to an absolute minimum.

Small-space gardening

Would-be gardeners with access only to a balcony or patio can try growing their crops in containers. These come in various shapes, sizes and materials, ranging from purpose-built terracotta or plastic pots, which are available from garden centres, to huge plastic tubs sold by specialist suppliers. For the more ecologically-minded gardeners, discarded items, such as bath tubs and sinks, can be recycled as miniature gardens.

Although growing plants in containers is not strictly 'organic', it is better to grow some vegetables for home use, even in a quasi-organic system, than to grow no vegetables at all. Your choice of growing media is critical for success, and only a high-quality compost, with any peat left out, will do (see page 36). There is less room for error in container gardening, and special attention must be paid to keeping the containers well watered and topped up with nutrients during the growing season.

Controlling weeds

Weeds are the bane of gardening life. Left to their own devices, they will out-compete crops for water, light and fertility, often leaving the less fastidious gardener with few vegetables to harvest.

Because they prefer undisturbed soil, biennial weeds are seldom a problem in a vegetable garden. The main culprits are the annual and perennial weeds, and they more than make up for the absence of their compatriot.

Annual weeds

Annual weeds, such as fat hen (*chenoparlium album*) and chickweed (*stellaria media*), will constantly regenerate from seed reserves in the soil. The population in the reserves is often huge, the result of neglected weeds being allowed to flower and shed seed. These seeds, although they are alive, are dormant and can remain in this state for several years.

Digging or hoeing the soil will break the dormancy of some of them, and a mob of weed seedlings will suddenly emerge. The remaining seeds stay dormant, biding their time until their turn comes to germinate.

Every effort should be made to prevent fresh seed from replenishing the numbers already there. This means that you should:
● Scrupulously remove all weeds before they shed their seed.
● Use only weed seed-free organic matter for mulching and soil improvement.
● Control annual weeds when they are still seedlings and cannot compete with the crops.

● Use rotations and mulches as powerful allies in the fight against annual weeds (see page 53), but employ other techniques, too, so that they work effectively.

Hoeing and hand weeding

Both hoeing and hand weeding are vital in the fight against weeds. They are the perfect partners that complement each other in a vegetable and herb garden. Hoes cut weeds off at ground level, efficiently controlling them where there is enough distance between plants (see page 54). Hand weeding is the only really effective method of weed control where space is a problem and is indispensable in crops such as carrots and parsnips, which have little space between the plants in a row.

Promoting crop competition

The crops themselves can be managed to improve their fighting chances to combat weeds. For example, you can try one of the following to promote competition:
● Transplanting or growing crops at equal spacings in order to smother weeds and keep their growth in check.
● Keeping poor competitors, such as onions, off weedy ground and substituting a strong competitor, such as potatoes.

Using stale seedbeds

Stale seed beds are used to give crop plants a head start over weeds. Prepare the bed a week or two before sowing to allow the weed seeds at the soil surface to germinate. Hoe off the seedlings or burn with a flame weeder to produce a stale seedbed ready for sowing.

Perennial weeds

Perennial weeds come back year after year from hardy roots and stems that endure both dry summers and cold winters. Some, like docks and dandelions, have deep taproots, while others, such as couch grass and stinging nettles, have a system of creeping roots or stems that spread throughout the garden.

Since they are masters of survival, perennial weeds are difficult to eradicate once they become established. Digging might get rid of them, but this is tedious and time-consuming and needs to be done thoroughly since new plants can regenerate from pieces left behind.

Hoeing and pulling off their top growth can bring temporary respite and could even weaken the plants and cause their death. Eradication, however, is difficult since the tops need to be regularly and frequently taken off for several years. Otherwise, any weeds that are missed can go on to live another day. Perennial weeds can also be controlled by mulches laid between the crop plants, but their tops often outgrow the mulch, and you will have to remove them before they get too big.

Many of the perennial weeds, such as docks, produce seed from which new plants can grow. Like annuals, you should never allow them to flower and set seed in your garden, although this cannot always keep seeds out. Some, like dandelions, can blow in from scrub ground or abandoned plots, and there is little or nothing that you can do about this.

If you are losing the fight against perennial weeds, then you may even have to consider surrendering the affected parts of the garden and covering them with a black plastic film. After two or three years in the dark, the weeds underneath should be dead, rescuing the area for vegetable and herb production.

Mulching

Covering the soil with a layer of material is called 'mulching'. This is a standard practice in organic gardening and an effective, chemical-free way of nourishing the soil. Use in cropped and non-cropped parts of the garden.

Use materials such as carpet, newspaper and lawn clippings – nothing goes to waste in the drive to mulch. In a vegetable garden, mulches are at their best nestled among the plants to check the growth of weeds, reduce water evaporation from the soil surface and promote earthworm activity. They protect the soil underneath from the ravages of heavy rains and insulate it against temperature extremes.

The temperature and moisture level of a mulched soil are slow to change, so apply mulches only when the soil is warm and moist. Unfortunately, slugs and snails love the moist environment underneath, and crop losses can be catastrophic if their populations build up. However, the pros outweigh the cons.

Bulking up

Bulky organic materials, such as compost, are a natural choice for mulching organic gardens. They not only add organic matter to the soil, but many of them are also a source of plant nutrients. Most, too, come from recycled garden and kitchen wastes and cost nothing to make. Organic mulching material should be weed-free and loose enough for air and water to pass through to the soil underneath. If using wood shavings and saw dust, they must come from untreated wood or they will contaminate the soil. They can deplete the soil of nitrogen and should be weathered in the open for a couple of years before using.

Spread bulky organic mulches thickly enough to do their job, but not so thick as to cover the crop plants. To some extent, thicker is better, though the ideal thickness varies with the crop; the material being used; and the quantities of mulch that are available.

Plastic mulches

You can buy opaque plastic films, custom-made for mulching. These petroleum-based products have few of the advantages of bulky organic mulches. They are better in annual rather than perennial crops, where they can be removed periodically to refreshen the soil.

You can also get plastic mulch from local dairy farmers who often use large sheets of black plastic to cover silage, replacing them as they wear out. Usually, the plastic still has some life left in it and can be used to cover a vegetable or herb bed. Lay it over a bed before sowing or planting and secure with soil stacked along its edges. Cut holes for the plants either before or after it is laid. You can sow, plant and water through the holes, which will need to be weeded until the crops get big enough to compete on their own.

Your site

Organic gardening is a series of individual activities which are linked together inextricably in a system that produces healthy food in an environmentally positive way. Two of the first acts that a gardener must perform are also the most critical – choosing a site and deciding on its size. You will have to make the most of what you've got, whether it's a smallholding or pots on a patio.

Size matters

Size does matter, and the ideal dimensions of a garden depend on how it will be used. If, for example, your main purpose is to grow food for your own consumption, then a plot the size of an allotment may be enough for a small family. Alternatively, a market garden being used to support a small box scheme may need to be a hectare or two in size, one part of which is growing vegetables and herbs, and the other part resting under a green manure.

Crop losses from weeds can be serious, so the size of a garden must be adjusted to what can realistically be kept clean. Although it is normal to want to start big, smaller is better until you hone your weed control skills enough to take on something larger.

A quality job

Since any shortcomings, however minor they seem at first, can become major irritations later, select only sites with specific qualities. Of all the possible places where it can go, a garden should at least be near home; next to a water supply; and away from strong winds or close to wind breaks. To grow productive crops, the site's soil also should be of a high standard (see opposite), although most deficiencies can, to some extent, be corrected.

Spaced out

Vegetables and herbs need room to grow, although how much room varies with a crop's ability to withstand crowding. For instance, salad onions are more tolerant than most

vegetables, and they can be squeezed in at a population of 100–200 plants per square metre. However, at the other extreme are Brussels sprouts, which succeed best when just one to four plants are grown per square metre.

The character of a crop depends on the density at which it is grown. Low beetroot populations produce large roots which are ideal for the show bench. Total yields, however, are sacrificed since the large sizes are not enough to make up for low plant numbers.

As the population is increased, the roots get correspondingly smaller, although the yields are increased as the plant numbers compensate for the small roots. At some point, however, populations are increased to the point where root size and yields begin to decline.

Designer rows

To get the highest yields, you need a good-sized vegetable plot with the plants spaced an equal distance from each other. This even distribution is ideal with widely-spaced crops that are weeded by hand or hoe, and works just as well for close-growing crops which are weeded by hand. It comes up short, however,

with tightly-packed crops that are hoed – the plants are simply too close together for the tools to get in between them.

To make room for hoes, change the pattern to leave the plants closer together within a row and further apart between the rows. The same population is maintained, but the wider-spaced rows allow a hoe to move in between the plants and do their job. Hand weeding is not eliminated since the plants within the row are still too close together for hoeing.

Water, water everywhere

From seed germination to harvest, water is absolutely essential for plant growth. It is, however, an increasingly scarce and expensive resource, and gardeners have a duty to manage it carefully.

Up in the air

Water in the garden is subject to a dynamic cycle of loss and renewal. For example, in plants, it continuously evaporates from the surfaces of leaves. Foraging roots, however, compensate for this by taking in soil water, which then works its way up to the leaves.

Soils are store houses of water that are continuously being depleted, not just by growing plants but also by evaporation directly into the air. Given this state of affairs, the soils would eventually dry out if they were not periodically replenished by rainfall or irrigation water.

Reducing water losses

- Decrease the crop population so that there are fewer plants competing for the same amount of water.
- Control weeds when they are young.
- Locate the vegetable plot in a sheltered spot to protect it from the wind.
- Establish wind breaks on windy sites.
- Work in green manures, compost and well-rotted manure to increase the soil's water-holding capacity.
- Mulch the soil to reduce evaporation from its surface.
- Utilize sub-soiling or, in small gardens, deep digging to increase the crop's rooting depth.

Evaporation

This is an on-going process that reaches its peak on a hot, sunny summer's day when the soil is moist and the wind is blowing. In order to combat water losses, frugal gardeners must go on the offensive and initiate preemptive strikes before the plants suffer (see box).

Time to water

Wherever you live, there will be times when there just is not enough rainfall, and even the thriftiest of gardeners will have to water. One of the most critical times for moisture is during crop establishment – never allow recently-sown seeds, newly-germinated seedlings and just-transplanted plants to dry out.

Watering established plants

As a general rule, you should try to water established plants heavily every once in a while rather than lightly all the time. Plants, however, are created differently and do not necessarily accept general rules. Leafy crops, like spinach and cabbage, respond to regular watering throughout their lives. Peas and beans will prefer less water before they flower, and more in the flowering to pod-swelling stage of their development. Similarly, root crops will need more water when their roots begin to swell.

Watering techniques

Watering established plants with sprinklers is a hit-or-miss affair which can be wasteful and ineffective – water is often blown around or evaporates before it hits the ground. Always apply water to the soil just above the plants' roots, where it can do the most good.

In small gardens, you can fit watering cans and hose pipes with attachments that deliver water directly to the plants. An option for small and large gardens is a drip irrigation system, consisting of black plastic tubing fitted with miniature nozzles. Water slowly drips from the nozzles and goes straight into the soil. The nozzles can be placed next to the plants. To reduce water losses even more, the whole irrigation system can go under a mulch.

Alternatively, porous hose pipes, which are purportedly made from recycled tyres, can be laid directly on the soil near the plants. Nozzles are not necessary since water oozes out of the entire length of the pipe.

What to grow

Gardening catalogues list about 30 or so well-known vegetables and about 10 commonly-grown herbs, with numerous minor crops thrown in for good measure. Although novice gardeners may be confused by such a jumble of plants, they need not despair; coming to their aid are various classification schemes that bring order to all the chaos.

Family ties

In a branch of botany called taxonomy, plants with similar characteristics are grouped together into families (see the table opposite). Developing an understanding of these family relationships is more than just an intellectual exercise. It is, instead, at the heart of rotation design since the same pests and diseases often attack members of the same family (see page 38).

For better or for worse, the taxonomists carry on classifying beyond the family level. They divide each family down into smaller groups which are called 'genera', with each genus sharing certain traits that distinguish it from other genera.

Genera are then divided further into 'species', each of which has its own special characteristics. Using this system, the genus and species names of beetroot, for example, are *Beta vulgaris*; runner beans are *Phaseolus coccineus*; and sweet corn is *Zea mays*.

Some like it hot

Based on their temperature preference and ability to tolerate cold conditions, vegetables and herbs can be divided into either warm season or cool season crops.

Warm season crops

These thrive in the summer heat and are easily injured or killed by frost. Most are partial to the warmth of a tunnel or greenhouse, and include among their numbers basil, French beans, courgettes and peppers.

Cool season crops

These crops can germinate and grow at cooler temperatures. Some are better adapted to the cold than others; many will survive a cold winter. The hardiest ones include kale, broad beans and onions, while at the other end of the scale are potatoes, whose tops die back in a heavy frost.

Flowering times

A plant's life cycle starts with seed germination; goes through a growth stage that continues into flowering and seed production; and finally ends in death. All flowering plants are classified into annuals, biennials and perennials, depending on the duration of their life cycles.

Annuals

These run through their life cycle within one growing season. Short-duration crops, such as coriander and lettuce, go to seed very quickly, and need constant resowing for an unbroken harvest of leaves. In contrast, French beans are long-season annuals, and those varieties that are grown for their dried seeds may not mature before the onset of winter, leaving behind soft, immature seeds unfit for storing.

Biennials

These flower, seed and die in their second season. Some leafy biennials, such as parsley and perpetual spinach, produce a continuous crop of leaves in their first year, finally stopping when they flower in the spring of the following year. Root crops, such as carrots and beetroot, are also biennial, although they are normally harvested before flowering.

Perennials

Perennials, such as globe artichokes and rosemary, live for a number of years before succumbing to the ravages of old age. Technically, peppers and tomatoes are also perennials, although in cold northern gardens they die each year as if they were annuals.

Family connections

Family current name (prior name)	Commonly grown vegetables and herbs	Less common vegetables and herbs
Alliaceae (*Amaryllidaceae*):	Leek, Onion, Shallot	Chives
Apiaceae (*Umbelliferae*):	Carrot, Coriander, Parsley, Parsnip	Celeriac, Celery, Fennel
Asteraceae (*Compositae*):	Lettuce	Chicory/Endive, Globe artichoke, Jerusalem artichoke, Salsify, Scorzonera
Brassicaceae (*Cruciferae*):	Broccoli/Calabrese, Brussels sprouts, Cabbage, Cauliflower, Kale, Chinese cabbage, Pak choi, Radish, Swede, Turnip	Kohlrabi, Texsel greens, Mizuna, Tatsoi
Chenopodiaceae:	Beetroot, Perpetual spinach, Spinach	New Zealand spinach
Cucurbitaceae:	Cucumber, Courgette	Pumpkin, Squash
Fabaceae (*Leguminosae*):	Broad Bean, French Bean, Runner Bean, Pea	Fenugreek
Lamiaceae (*Labiatae*):	Basil, Marjoram, Mint, Oregano, Rosemary, Thyme	–
Liliaceae:	–	Asparagus
Poaceae (*Gramineae*):	Sweet corn	Lemon grass
Solanaceae:	Pepper, Potato, Tomato	Aubergine, Tomatillo

Selection criteria

A 'variety' in gardening terms is a group of plants within a species which is distinguished by certain characteristics, such as size and colour. The red 'Crimson Globe' beetroot, for example, differs in colour from the yellow 'Burpee's Golden'. Both are beetroots, yet their traits separate them into different varieties.

A flip through the gardening catalogues reveals there are thousands of vegetable and herb varieties. With crops like tomatoes running well into the hundreds, selection is not easy. If you are on the lookout for something new, you need a clear-cut idea of what you want.

Quality and quantity

To make your work worthwhile, you should go for high-yielding varieties, especially those with pest and disease resistance. The quest for yields can also be coupled with a search for flavour, although in the real world the two may not always feature in the same variety.

The older the better

Also worth looking at are the so-called 'heritage' varieties that have been handed down from generation to generation of gardeners. Although they have their staunch supporters, there also are detractors who claim that they can be challenging to grow; their yields can be disappointingly low; and they have no more to offer than their modern equivalents. Despite the negative reviews, they are great fun to have around, both for their historical value and the novelty of their eccentric shapes, sizes and colours.

Modern times

Competing with the heritage varieties for catalogue space are the modern hybrid varieties. Bred for their uniformity, they are good yielders of high-quality crops which are often resistant to pests and diseases. Despite their advantages, hybrids have not taken over completely. Modern non-hybrids are still being bred for yield, quality and pest and disease resistance. They have an important place in the garden, since some, such as peas and French beans, are available only as non-hybrids.

Going organic

Although organic seed is becoming more readily available in catalogues, the varieties on offer may not necessarily be the best performers. Whether to use organic seed or not will depend on your philosophical commitment and, in the case of certified holdings, the current status of the EU organic regulation. Daring gardeners can have a go at saving their own 'organic' seed. Simple though it may seem, this can be a tricky proposition which is fraught with problems:

• Only mature seed should be collected.
• Don't save seeds of hybrids since they will not come back true to type.
• Seed-borne diseases and cross-pollination between varieties must be controlled.
• Biennials, e.g. carrots and beetroot, require two years' work before harvesting any seed.
• Completely dry the seed before storing.

Once these problems are sorted out, however, seed saving will become a satisfying part of your gardening life which makes a connection with both the past and the future.

Protecting your crops

Protected cropping has its detractors, who usually cite the use of non-renewable plastics as the reason for their disapproval. They have a point, but growing your vegetables under cover is so appealing that it is relatively easy to succumb to its temptations.

Trapping warmth

Protected cropping uses specialized materials, such as fleeces, and structures, such as tunnels, to trap the sun's warmth and shield growing plants from the wind. The temperatures around the plants are boosted, thereby forcing spring crops to come on earlier and autumn harvests to go on longer.

Over-wintering oriental greens, turnips and coriander will flourish in this environment, while the tropical immigrants, such as peppers and aubergines, find the extra heat invaluable. The protective environment is also ideal for starting transplants, particularly of warm-season crops, such as tomatoes and peppers.

Take care

However, cropping under cover is not trouble free, and the conditions inside can go to dangerous extremes – on sunny, summer days, temperatures can reach life-threatening highs. With most types of protected cropping, rainfall cannot get in, and therefore drought is a constant threat. However, some conscientious venting and watering will usually solve these potential problems, although these options are not always possible if your garden is located some distance away from your home.

Making the right choice

Styles of protected cropping vary in their design, cost and effectiveness. With so much choice, there is something to suit every garden and small holding, whatever the size.

Fleeces

Soft, lightweight fleeces are draped loosely over a crop like a blanket. They are particularly good for bringing on over-wintered salads and encouraging the growth of early potatoes, lettuces and carrots. Because the crops are completely enclosed, some pests are also kept at bay. To stop them from blowing away, fasten down the fleeces with pegs, bricks, tyres or lengths of wood. They are pocked with small holes, so rainfall easily penetrates to the soil underneath. Unfortunately, they have a short shelf life, though with care they should last at least two or three seasons.

Garden frames

These are low-lying square or rectangular structures with movable tops that provide ventilation and access to the inside. Garden centres and catalogues sell different models, but DIY enthusiasts may want to take on the challenge and build their own.

Making a garden frame is not rocket science, and you can use a range of materials to get one up and running. The sides, for example, can be made from bricks, breeze blocks or plywood sheets, while anything that lets in the light, such as recycled shower doors and double-glazed windows, can be used for the tops. Another approach is to stretch a plastic film over a wooden frame, producing a light structure which is moved around easily.

Greenhouses and tunnels

These are large walk-in structures that usually come with big price tags. They play the same role in the garden, but go about it in different ways. Greenhouses are made of sheets of glass or stiff polycarbonate plastic supported by wooden or aluminium frames. They are fiddly to erect, although their longevity is more than fair compensation for this shortcoming.

Tunnels are less sophisticated and amount to little more than a row of metal hoops covered with a plastic sheet. This simplicity means that they are easier to erect and, for the area they cover, cheaper to buy. Unlike greenhouse glass, the plastic sheet eventually surrenders to the destructive effects of sunlight, disintegrating after four or five years of use. The hoops get hot under the summer sun, causing the sheet to wear out more quickly where the two touch. You can stick 'anti-hot spot' tape, a foam-like material, on the outsides of the hoops to insulate the plastic from the hot metal, adding at least an extra year or two to its life.

If you are intimidated by the cost of new tunnels and greenhouses, then you can try

Where to site a greenhouse or a tunnel

Tunnels and greenhouses cannot go just anywhere, and you must judge any potential garden sites carefully for their ability to accommodate them. You will need to take the following points into consideration when selecting a suitable location for tunnels and greenhouses.

● Slope: The site for a greenhouse should either be level or flat enough to be easily levelled off. A tunnel is another matter and can be erected on either sloping or on level land.

● Size of the area: The site should be big enough to accommodate not only the structure but also a strip of ground running along its four sides. The strip should be wide enough – 1 m (3 ft) or more – to provide you with easy access for repairing, washing and changing the glass and plastic.

● Shade: Both greenhouses and tunnels should be kept away from any trees, buildings and fences that might shade the plants inside.

● Distance from the house: Watering and venting will be easier with greenhouses and tunnels located near the house.

buying cheaper second-hand versions. Local newspapers and notice boards often advertise bargains but always proceed with caution.

In the case of tunnels, check the hoops for rust, and inspect any plastic included in the deal for tears, holes and scratches. Buying second-hand greenhouses requires the same due diligence, such as looking for broken glass, rotting wood and bent aluminium.

Vegetable cropping schemes in tunnels

Vegetable	Dates*	
	In**	Out
Carrots	October	May/Early June
Peppers or cucumbers	May/Early June	October
Dwarf sugar snap peas	October	April
Tomatoes or courgettes	April	October
Leaves***	October	April
Climbing French beans	April	September
Tall sugar snap peas	January	July
Courgettes	July	October
Carrots or dwarf sugar snap peas	January	Early June
Peppers or cucumbers	Early June	October

* Vary according to part of country and weather conditions.
** Assumes all except carrots and peas are started as transplants.
*** Includes Oriental greens, parsley, perpetual spinach, chicory and endive.

Maintenance

Tunnels and greenhouses are high-maintenance structures which need mollycoddling to work. You must water the crops inside diligently and wash off any algae regularly. In addition, ventilation through the doors and, in the case of greenhouses, roof vents, is compulsory.

Cropping plan

Although greenhouses and tunnels are ideal for growing summer crops, such as tomatoes and peppers, they are just as dependable for producing a wide range of winter vegetables and herbs. As if made for each other, winter and summer plantings can be matched into useful cropping schemes that produce edibles for a good part of the year (see above).

Cloches

These have a long and honoured history in the vegetable garden. Modern versions are often lightweight plastic structures that can be shifted around easily. The simplest ones of all are bell-shaped designs that cover individual plants or pots, whereas others are reminiscent of miniature tunnels which straddle sections of beds and rows.

The only disadvantage of using cloches to protect your crops is their tendency to fly away in very strong winds. To prevent this, they can, of course, be anchored to the ground. However, if your site for growing vegetables is excessively windy, it might be better to ban them completely and to choose another protective method instead.

Vegetative propagation

Vegetative propagation uses plant parts other than seeds to produce offspring. Although this method is used on only a few vegetables, such as potatoes and garlic, it comes into its own with perennial herbs, especially those whose seeds are sterile or produce off-type plants. There are several effective techniques of vegetative propagation that are easy to use, although none of them works equally well on all herbs.

Division

Herbs that grow in clumps can be dug up, then divided into pieces and replanted directly into the garden soil.

Root cuttings

Some herbs are propagated by root cuttings taken in autumn or early spring. Grow the pieces of root in a well-drained compost until new plants develop.

Stem cuttings

You can regenerate new plants from stem cuttings taken from a parent plant. Root the cuttings in trays of propagating compost, then transplant either into pots or a spot in the garden. Stem cuttings vary, according to the age of the stem and the season in which they are taken:
• Softwood cuttings come from young growth in spring to early summer.
• Semi-hardwood cuttings are taken from half-ripened stems in the period from summer to early autumn.
• Hardwood cuttings are made from mature stems in the autumn.

Layering

This produces new plants while they are still attached to the parent plant. In one type of layering which is suitable for herbs, you need to single out a strong, flexible stem for propagation. Cut a slice from the underside of the stem and then bend it over and down so that the cut side comes into contact with the soil. To keep it in place, just peg down the stem with a loop of wire and then cover with soil to encourage root growth. Leave the tip uncovered – this will become the stem of the new plant. When the new plant is ready, you can cut it off and either pot it up or move to its permanent site.

Growing herbs

It is very satisfying to grow your own herbs organically. Not only will they taste better than their supermarket counterparts but also you can pick them fresh whenever you need them and can indulge yourself in growing a range of different and unusual varieties.

Culinary and medicinal

Since a little bit goes a long way, only a few plants of each herb are needed for kitchen use. Most grow well in containers, making them ideal for gardens that are confined to a patio or other limited space, such as a roof garden or even a window box. Of course, if you are interested in complementary medicine and natural therapies, you may consider growing your own herbs for their medicinal and therapeutic properties. Herbs can also be an important ingredient in many cosmetics and beauty preparations. For more information on this, turn to page 176.

Basil

Basil has strong associations with the cooking of warm climates, and both Italian and Thai food would not be the same without it. It is a frost-sensitive annual that hits its stride in the cloistered environment of a greenhouse or tunnel. The catalogues have an interesting selection of varieties, and a good one to start with is 'Genovese', or sweet basil, which is excellent in tomato sauces and pesto. 'Siam Queen' will appeal to lovers of Thai food, while gardeners looking for something more ornate can try the purple-leafed 'Ruben'.

Chives

This hardy perennial has an onion-like flavour which is common to the other members of its family. The thin, hollow leaves of chives are snipped with scissors and added as a flavouring to soups, salads and omelettes, while its edible flowers add colour and flavour to salads.

You can grow chives from seed or by dividing established plants. Although they prefer a sunny spot with fertile, moist soil, they can tolerate some shade and drought. You can even grow them in small pots on the kitchen window sill, ready to snip whenever the need arises.

Coriander

This increasingly popular herb has a very distinctive scent and flavour. Coriander has become an indispensable ingredient in many Indian, Mexican and Thai dishes.

Given a sunny and well-drained site, it can be grown outdoors from spring until autumn, even in northern climates. Take care because coriander quickly runs to seed, especially during the heat of summer, and to guarantee an uninterrupted supply of leaves, you should sow it continuously throughout the year, preferably using a good leaf-producing variety such as 'Santo'.

Mint

Mint is one of the most commonly used culinary herbs and it is really easy to grow. Mints prefer a moist, fertile soil, and can tolerate some shade. Beware as they can soon colonize a garden with their underground shoots. You can control them by consigning the plants to a large pot or bath tub, or by dividing them every two or three years.

Mints come in different disguises: they are sometimes decorated with variegated leaves; are occasionally shrunken in size; and often are identified by names that reflect their flavour, including spearmint, chocolate mint, apple mint, lemon mint and peppermint.

Vegetative propagation is by means of division, root cuttings or soft wood cuttings (see page 65), although the best technique will vary with the type of mint.

Parsley

Parsley comes in two versions: flat and curly. Both are biennials that go to seed the year after they are sown. They prefer a moist, fertile soil, and grow well in either full sun or partial shade. Since the seeds are slow to germinate, it is better to start parsley off as transplants. Sow in an unheated tunnel or greenhouse in early spring, then put out in late spring or early summer. You can also do a later sowing for over-wintering in an unheated tunnel or greenhouse.

Unless intended for commercial production, there is little point in growing curly parsley; it just is not as well-flavoured as the flat-leafed type. The catalogues, however, carry only a limited number of flat-leafed cultivars.

Rosemary

The stiff, pointed leaves of rosemary are natural additions to tomato sauces and roast lamb. The plants are evergreen shrubs that like a well-drained, chalky soil in full sun. Despite their woody nature and tough appearance, they are not the hardiest of herbs, finding cold, wet winters disagreeable.

Although the erect, upright varieties are more common, there are also prostrate ones that look particularly attractive cascading down a stone wall. You can propagate them by layering or taking soft-wood and semi-hardwood cuttings (see page 65).

Sage

Sage is a perennial evergreen shrub that needs sun and a well-drained soil. The hardy common sage is strongly flavoured and the type most often used in cooking. If you want something a little off the wall, then why not try pineapple sage, a cold frost-hardy type with pineapple-scented leaves? Sage can be vegetatively propagated by taking either softwood or semi-hardwood cuttings (see page 65). Common sage can also be propagated by layering.

Thyme

This herb is at its best in a well-drained, sunny site, where it grows as a woody, evergreen perennial which needs some pruning to be at its best. Although common thyme is perhaps the most familiar type in the garden, do not overlook its lemon-scented partner. Thymes are vegetatively propagated by division, and by taking softwood or semi-hardwood cuttings.

Harvesting your crops

Harvests are the rewards of the gardener's labour. The reward comes quickly with crops such as summer radish, which are ready for picking within 20–30 days from sowing. However, others, like sprouting broccoli, are less forthcoming, with some varieties taking up to ten or eleven months before they can be harvested and eaten.

Poorly-timed harvests can ruin a crop. Those made too soon produce inedible vegetables, such as thin, anaemic carrots and tiny, watery peas. But if the harvests are taken too late, the results are at best compost fodder that no one wants to eat, like flowering calabrese, seedy ridge cucumbers and tough French beans.

Flexible harvesting

As long as the extremes of age are avoided, harvest times for most vegetables are flexible. Courgettes, for example, can be picked small or can stay on the plant to become marrows. Likewise, bulbing onions can be pulled young for salads or left to grow to their full size. Pepper fruits, too, can be picked when they are an immature green or a ripe red colour.

Survival crops

Hardy crops, like winter cabbage and leeks, can survive the winter in the garden. Cold temperatures refrigerate them on the spot, stretching out their harvest periods for months. In a well-drained soil, root vegetables, such as carrots and parsnips, can also stay put, although they may need a covering of straw to keep off freezing temperatures.

Storing your crop

Once they are harvested, vegetables and herbs will soon start to lose their flavour and texture. If they cannot be eaten immediately, as often happens when you have a glut, then the more perishable ones, such as cauliflowers, lettuce and parsley, can be kept for a short time in the refrigerator.

Durable vegetables, such as bulbing onions, winter squashes and potatoes, can be stored for months in a dry, well-ventilated barn or shed, where they will be well protected from freezing temperatures.

Onions must always be dried down before they go into store, and the squashes should be picked with their stems still attached to the fruit. Potatoes must be kept in the dark so they do not turn green and bitter, and should be stored in either heavy-duty paper sacks or bins, covered with a blanket.

Obviously, if you have the time and enjoy cooking, you can preserve many vegetables by blanching and freezing them or by bottling and pickling. Some are very versatile indeed: tomatoes, for example, can be dried in the sun, bottled in olive oil, or made into sauces and bottled or frozen until required.

Pests and diseases

There are a discouraging number of pests and diseases that can attack vegetables but only a few of them become problems in any one year. Although something can usually be salvaged from even the most desperate-looking crop, damage must be kept to a minimum so that all your hard work in the garden is not wasted.

Knowing the enemy

Pests are animals that attack crops, and they include mammals as large as deer and as small as moles and mice; birds such as pigeons; all manner of insects from larvae to adults; slugs and snails; mites; and microscopic nematodes. They suck, chew and burrow through seeds, seedlings and mature plants.

Diseases are microscopic parasites that live off plants. Also known as pathogens, they are made up of bacteria, fungi and viruses. They move around on seeds and transplants; some can live in the soil for years. Fungi and bacteria are blown around by the wind, while viruses are often transported by sap-sucking aphids.

Prevention and cure

Total control over pests and diseases is neither possible nor necessary in an organic garden. Your goal should be damage limitation, using techniques that maintain a balance between your needs and those of the environment.

From the ground up

Producing fit and healthy plants is the first line of defence against pests and diseases. You can achieve this only if the site and soil are suitable for crop production, and any deficiencies must be corrected before growing begins.

Composts are magic elixirs, and applying them to soils can help suppress or control diseases. However, they must never become a source of infection themselves, and plant material infected by persistent soil-borne diseases, such as allium white rot and brassica club root, should not go into the compost heap.

Well-designed rotations help promote a healthy soil. To be most effective, you should plan them so that plants of the same family are grown on a different piece of ground each year (see page 38).

Keep it clean

A clean garden is a healthy garden, and paying close attention to basic hygiene will bring dividends.
- Thoroughly wash your boots, gardening tools and equipment, which can all be carriers of soil-borne pests and diseases, before moving from one garden to another.
- Clean up crop debris and weeds.
- Use only disease-free seed and planting material, including transplants and potato tubers, to start a crop.

Protecting your crops

You can protect your vegetables and herbs from many common pests and diseases just by taking a few simple, time-honoured precautions. Here are some suggestions and guidelines for you to try out in your vegetable plot.

● Remove any winter vegetables before starting to plant your spring ones. Overwintered vegetables can act as hosts to some pests and diseases which can then spread to spring-grown crops. For example, winter brassicas can be a source of aphids and whiteflies.

● Grow your crops at wider-than-normal row spacing in order to promote better air movement through the canopy and help keep disease levels down. Diseases can also build up in stagnant air surrounding vegetables and herbs.

● Vent your tunnels and greenhouses, even during the winter months, to renew and refreshen the air inside.

● Adjust your sowing and harvest times to avoid pests and diseases. For instance, carrots are attacked by early and late generations of carrot root fly, so you should delay sowing main crop varieties until June in order to miss the first generation. Potatoes, too, are more likely to avoid blight damage if you grow early-maturing varieties.

● Use resistant vegetable varieties in your fight against pests and diseases. You should always choose them carefully to reduce the damage of blight in potatoes, root fly in carrots, rust in leeks and mildew in lettuce.

Barriers

You can use physical barriers to keep pests away from vegetable and herb crops. Home-cut circles or squares of carpet foam put at the base of brassica plants will keep out cabbage root fly. Likewise, a wall of plastic sheeting, mesh or fleece about 45 cm (18 in) high can be erected around the carrot patch to protect it against carrot root fly.

Fine mesh nets, reminiscent of mosquito netting, make a versatile and easy-to-use barrier for large and small areas. Laid over a crop, they are good all-rounders that deter deer, pigeons, and flying insects. They can even keep the dreaded flea beetle away from brassicas if put down as soon as a crop is sown.

Natural-born killers

Predators and parasites of pests live naturally in and around the garden. These 'beneficials' include birds, hover flies, ladybirds and lacewings, quietly going about their business of killing off any pests and keeping their populations down. You can encourage more of these beneficials to come into your garden by doing the following.

● Put up hospitable nesting boxes and provide safe havens where garden birds can live and nurture their young.

● Grow flowering plants, like phacelia and Michaelmas daisy, to lure in the smaller beneficials, such as hover flies.

● Create habitats to provide these silent allies with an overwintering refuge from which they can attack pests during the following growing season. These habitats can be simple, home-made affairs, such as some flower pots loosely packed with straw, which will provide shelter for ladybirds and lacewings.

Specialist companies now us offer an ever-increasing selection of natural enemies of pests. These biological control agents include the pathogenic bacteria *Bacillus thuringiensis,* which kill caterpillars in cabbages and Brussels sprouts; parasitic nematodes which are used against soil-borne slugs; and also parasitic wasps which can be released in tunnels and greenhouses to control whitefly.

Given the right environment, these control agents will effectively keep pest populations in a vegetable garden down to an acceptable level, although they work best in the early stages of a pest attack.

Mixing things up

Interplanting or mixed planting is often promoted as a method of pest and disease control, but most of the recommended combinations fall into the realm of old wives' tales and are supported with little concrete evidence that justifies their use. However, some stand up to closer scrutiny and might actually work:

● French marigolds may keep whitefly out of greenhouses and tunnels
● Onions grown with carrots might reduce carrot root fly damage
● A mix of resistant and susceptible lettuce varieties seems to protect against downy mildew. Interplanting is worth trying, but only if you approach it with an open mind and enjoy a trial-and-error approach to gardening.

Physical removal

Pests and diseases can be physically removed to prevent their spread in the garden. Pulling out infected plants slows the movement of disease to unaffected areas, while crushing aphids between the fingers or washing them off with a hose pipe will work well when infestations are small. Caterpillars, slugs and snails can all be picked off plants.

Biocides

Organic gardening accepts the use of a limited number of biocides, including copper-based chemicals as fungicides and some plant extracts as insecticides. Although biocides are believed to be user-friendly, they are toxins and are not the ideal solution to pest and disease problems. Used incorrectly, they can pollute water courses and drift onto neighbouring gardens. Even when used correctly, they have a damaging influence since copper chemicals can harm earthworms, and insecticides can kill the natural enemies of pests as well as the pests themselves.

The use of biocides, even those acceptable in organic systems, is subject to Pesticides Safety Directorate regulations. This means that traditional plant-based formulations made at home are illegal, and commercial products are subject to strict controls. Using some biocides, such as copper and derris, has to be justified to the certifying body before any applications are made to certified crops. Given the legal constraints and their environmental impact, their role in an organic garden should be seen for what it is: a desperate measure to be employed only after everything else has failed.

Fruit

If you think that it's impossible to feed yourself with home-grown fruit, then think again. Many gardeners, even those with small gardens, produce enough fruit for the whole year. Simple home preservation and storage techniques, such as freezing, bottling, juicing, drying or jam-making, make fruit available even when it is out of season. Once your fruit is growing well, it does not need a great deal of attention, so it gives a very good return for the time you spend on it and will continue to yield for years to come. Although the exotic fruits, such as bananas, pineapples and oranges, may be off-limits, the many fruits that can be grown in temperate climates are delicious and nutritious. And you don't need a large garden either: walls and fences can be used as a growing area and produce a surprising amount of fruit in a small space.

Growing your own fruit

Nothing compares with organically home-grown fruit. For health, quality, flavour and sheer lusciousness, it wins hands-down over shop-bought fruit, which has often been sprayed with a cocktail of pesticides, treated with substances to prolong its shelf life and waxed to improve its appearance. Growing fruit yourself is not difficult and you don't need a smallholding or an orchard to harvest good crops of soft fruit and top fruit.

Gardening with nature

The healthiest way to grow fruit, for you, your garden and the environment, is to grow it organically. If you are used to being able to reach for quick-fix sprays to solve your garden pest and disease problems, you may be feeling apprehensive about giving them up. However, once you go organic you will find that you are managing your garden in a different way. Instead of fire-fighting problems as they occur, you will be using techniques that should prevent them happening, and you will learn to be automatically vigilant, spotting problems early on so that they do not get out of hand. You will be gardening with nature, rather than fighting against it.

This does not mean, however, that you will be plagued with problems. Experience teaches the organic gardener that an organic garden achieves a natural balance which means that pests and diseases are not usually serious. The chances of an all-out infestation are reduced

WARNING

Never replant any kind of fruit on a site where it was previously grown. Diseases may be present in the soil. Apple trees planted in the position where others have been growing may suffer from re-plant disease and will eventually die.

when the friendly insects, which devour pests, are encouraged. Using 'wholefood' compost and manures rather than 'fast food' bagged fertilizer produces stronger crops which are not overfed. This makes them less appealing to pests and better able to fight off disease. Fungal diseases are less prevalent when the soil is well managed and mulches are used. These techniques are explained later in more detail in this chapter.

Which varieties?

Fruit is divided into two groups: soft fruit and top fruit. Soft fruit is generally low growing and has a limited life-span. Top fruit, or tree fruit, could crop for a life-time. Rhubarb, although it is technically a stem vegetable, has been included as it is a useful early-season crop which most people regard as a fruit.

If flavour is very important to you, it will pay to taste different varieties of every type of fruit before you decide which ones to buy and plant. Ask your friends for their opinions and advice, or go to 'Pick Your Own' farms or farmers' markets and sample what's on offer.

Siting your fruit

Most types of top fruit and soft fruit can be grown free standing or trained against a wall or fence. The warmth and light available will vary depending on the aspect of the garden and its fences. An open, sunny position is best for fruit, but Morello cherries, gooseberries and currants should succeed in a north-facing position with little sun. Where space is really limited, try growing strawberries in tubs, or seek out miniature fruit varieties, which are designed to be grown on a sunny patio.

Sourcing bushes and trees

Although container-grown fruit plants from garden centres are acceptable and usually grow well, it can be cheaper, and there are more varieties to choose from, to buy bare-rooted plants from a specialist nursery. This usually entails using a mail order service and will mean planting in the dormant season between November and March. An increasing number of nurseries are offering organically grown fruit plants and bushes. Get a range of catalogues to find out what's available.

The soil

It is important to find out about your soil when you move to a new plot, or to test your soil in an existing plot if you are not sure of its characteristics. Simple testing kits, which will tell you how alkaline or acid your soil is, are easy to find in garden centres. Your soil will influence which fruits you can grow successfully.

If you are embarking on a large fruit-growing operation, it may be worth spending money on a professional test which will give you a detailed picture of the mineral and humus content of your soil.

You can modify the acidity or alkalinity to some extent, but there is no point trying to turn a very acid or very alkaline soil into a neutral one. You must learn to grow the fruit that is likely to thrive on the site you have. Most fruit prefers a slightly acid soil, but will tolerate neutral or slightly alkaline conditions. Raspberries, however, dislike alkaline soil.

You will need a supply of garden compost or well-rotted manure to feed the soil, especially if it is stony or very sandy (see page 31), and you may need rock phosphate, potash and, if you have no moral objections, fish, blood and bone, bonemeal or hoof and horn meal to correct any deficiencies.

Mulching

This is a useful technique if you grow soft fruit. A mulch conserves moisture, suppresses weeds and thereby cuts down on labour and water bills. It can also help with pest and disease control. It consists of a layer of organic material or a sheet of purpose-designed plastic or fabric laid over the soil. Purpose-designed woven or non-woven mulches have an advantage over a simple layer of black polythene because they are semi-permeable: they will let water through to your plants. They can stay in place for several years and are particularly useful for strawberries.

The disadvantage of plastic mulches is that they are not particularly pleasant to look at and, because they are permanent, the soil is starved of its natural contact with the air. In practice, this is not too much of a problem.

If you live in the country, newspaper and straw make a good and relatively cheap mulch for soft fruit. Ideally use organic straw, but this is unlikely to be available because organic farmers tend to need all their straw. The alternative is to buy conventionally produced bales at least six months before you intend to use them and weather them in a stack to remove possible pesticide residues.

When to mulch

These temporary organic mulches should be laid in late spring or early summer when the soil is warm and moist. Save newspapers and lay them, full thickness and overlapped to exclude all the light, around the roots of your fruit. Leave the mulch in place all summer, but remove and compost it in the autumn. This allows the birds access to any soil-dwelling pests. If you have chickens, let them scratch around the roots of your plants once the mulch is removed. They are great pest controllers, but check they don't make too many dust bath excavations and kill the fruit.

Preparing the site

It really does pay to prepare your site properly. Make sure you remove all weeds, including the perennials – there is no acceptable organic herbicide. Covering the ground with black plastic or cardboard for six to twelve months works well and cuts down on hand work.

Rotovating is slightly faster but only suitable on areas where there is enough space for a machine to work and turn. It can be used in late spring and summer. Rotovating soil filled with perennial weed roots sounds crazy as every piece of the root of a perennial weed has the potential to re-grow. However, if it is repeated up to four times just as the weeds start to grow again, it can eliminate them. Rotovation must be carried out in dry weather. You could use a rotovator to break up new ground and follow it with very careful hand-digging. On small areas, hand-digging alone may work, but you will need to start well before planting time so that any fragments of perennial weed roots have a chance to re-grow and be removed during further cultivations.

Notes on pruning

Pruning fruit trees and bushes is necessary for several reasons:
- Diseased branches need to be removed at an early stage to prevent the infection from spreading.
- Pruning improves air circulation around the remaining branches, and prevents them from rubbing against, and injuring, each other. Wounds provide an entry point for pests and diseases.
- Pruning maintains or increases the yield of fruit you are likely to get – it is essential to prune the berry fruits for this reason.
- It shapes the tree or bush so it is balanced and pleasing to look at.
Note: A specialist book will show you how to prune, but the easiest way of learning is to attend a short course or demonstration.

Soft fruit

This includes all the cane and berry fruits as well as strawberries. Soft fruit tolerates most types of soil, but it prefers slightly acid conditions. You don't need a large garden to harvest your own delicious soft fruit.

It's possible to grow soft fruit in a very small garden, especially if you are prepared to use the space against a wall or fence. Strawberries can be grown in pots, but the bush and cane fruits need to be grown in soil.

Support for soft fruit

Raspberries, tayberries and loganberries will need support. A fence with strong existing posts can be adapted using straining bolts and strong wire. Otherwise you will need to put up strong free-standing posts with similar bolts and wires. The posts should not be pressure treated but painted with an environmentally benign wood preservative. Gooseberries, redcurrants and white currants can be trained (see pages 86 and 87). Trained specimens need similar support to cane fruits. Strawberries and blackcurrants do not need support.

Bare-rooted plants

All bare-rooted soft fruit, including strawberries, needs roughly the same care when it arrives. You will receive a bundle of carefully wrapped, unpromising looking, sticks, with straggly roots and a set of planting instructions. Do not plant if the weather is frosty; everything should survive for a day or two in their wrappings. As soon as possible, open them up and soak overnight in a bucket of water to ensure the roots have taken up as much moisture as they need. Plant them immediately after soaking.

If they cannot be put in their permanent planting place, plants can be 'heeled in' for a few weeks. Heeling in involves laying the plants at an angle in a shallow trench and covering the roots with soil. The roots will start to grow but won't become anchored, and the plants will be easy to lift for the final planting (see instructions under each fruit).

Harvesting soft fruit

Always harvest soft fruit when the weather and the fruit are dry. Damp fruit will not taste as it should and will go mouldy very quickly. If you have to pick during damp weather, use the fruit immediately. All soft fruit, with the exception of gooseberries, has a very short shelf-life, even if it is refrigerated. Use it as soon as you can, or process it for storage on the day on which it is picked.

> ### Container-grown plants
> These can be planted at any time of year. However, remember that they will need plenty of watering if you are planting them in the summer.

Raspberries

Summer fruiting raspberries seem to be everyone's favourite, and in a good year 15 to 20 plants should satisfy a small family's cravings for raspberries and cream and allow for freezing some of the crop or bottling and jam-making. Add another row of a different variety and a short row of autumn raspberries as an insurance policy for a light cropping year.

Raspberries will tolerate some shade but are best in an east- or west- facing situation as they need sun for at least half the day. They can crop from late June to mid August, so you also need to take note of fruiting times when you are choosing them. It sounds obvious, but if you always go on holiday in August do not go for the later fruiting varieties.

Varieties

Commonly available varieties like Glen Moy are hardy and yield well. Malling Leo has a wonderful flavour, but it can take longer to establish. New varieties are introduced quite frequently. Never be tempted to take on young raspberry canes from a friend's garden. The canes that you buy from nurseries or from garden centres will be certified free from disease, and it is well worth starting with the best plants you can buy.

Autumn raspberries, which may begin fruiting almost as soon as their summer cousins finish, yield less heavily but they have a lovely flavour. Autumn Bliss is the most common late-fruiting variety, but some people prefer the more unusual golden-fruited varieties, such as Allgold.

Supports

There are several different methods of training raspberries of which the simplest and most economical, as far as space is concerned, involves planting the canes in a single row between strong 2.5 m (8 ft) long posts driven around 60 cm (2 ft) into the ground and set at around 3 m (10 ft) intervals. Wires are attached at 60 cm (2 ft), 90 cm (3 ft) and 150 cm (5 ft) from the ground. Straining bolts at one end of the row allow for the wires to be adjusted – they will loosen over time. The canes are tied in on one side of the wire after pruning in late summer. This prevents wind damage. Autumn fruiting raspberries do not need any support.

Planting

The weed-free soil, which you have previously prepared (see page 51), should be well dug, with home-made compost or well-rotted farmyard manure added at the recommended rate of one builder's wheelbarrow per 10 sq m. The raspberry canes should be planted 38–45 cm (15–18 in) apart. If you are planting more than one row, allow for a 2 m (6 ft) space between the rows; do not be tempted to skimp this distance. Plant at the depth at which the plants were growing in the nursery. Spread the roots out carefully and firm the plants in well. Cut back any canes that are planted in winter to around 22–30 cm (9–12 in) if they have not been cut back already by the nursery. They should grow away in the spring. Even though you will be severely tempted, try not to let them bear fruit in their first year – you must remove any flowers. They will not need a lot of attention, but they will require an adequate supply of water if the weather is particularly dry.

Pruning

With summer fruiting raspberries, at planting reduce the canes to between 15–20 cm (6–9 in). During the first season there is no need to prune. In the second year, cut out the canes that have fruited. These are generally easy to spot, as they begin to die back. Tie the new growth into the wires. You can fold over the tips of the shoots and secure them to the wires. At the end of the winter, shorten the canes by about 15 cm (6 in), cutting just above a healthy bud.

With autumn fruiting raspberries, all you have to do is simply cut the whole lot down to a few inches above ground level in February.

Raspberries are shallow rooted and produce new canes along the root run, so they often try to escape from the space that you have allotted to them. Be ruthless and weed them out if you want to keep them within bounds. Autumn raspberries are particularly prone to wandering. Mulches do help to keep the suckers, also known as 'spawn', in check.

Harvesting

Raspberries need picking almost every day. They are harvested without the stalk or the 'plug' which is inside the berry. Like all soft fruit, they should be picked when the weather and the fruit are dry. Damp fruit, which is picked in damp conditions, loses its texture and flavour and goes mouldy very quickly. Use your harvest, or process it, as soon as possible, or store in a single layer in a cool room, or the fridge, for a day.

Feeding

Feed raspberries only once a year in spring with compost or well-rotted manure at a rate of one builder's wheel barrow per 10 sq m (33 sq ft).

Blackberries and hybrids

You will need fewer plants of these types of soft fruit because they yield well and will take up a good deal of space in your garden.

The hybrid berries (loganberries, tayberries and boysenberries) are crosses between different berries within the species. They enjoy full sun, but also thrive on a west-facing wall or fence. Blackberries are less fussy and will grow against an east- or north-facing wall or fence.

Planting

Canes planted in winter should be cut back at planting to around 22 cm (9 in). They need to be planted 4–5 m (12–15 ft) apart if they are vigorous and 2.5–3 m (8–10 ft) apart if they are less strong growing. Incorporate manure or compost at the rate recommended for raspberries (see page 82) at planting time.

Support

Posts need to be erected in the same way as raspberry supports, but they need to be taller: 3 m (10 ft) long with 60 cm (2 ft) buried. Position four wires at intervals, with the lowest at 1 m (3 ft) and the highest at 2 m (6 ft) from the soil level. You could also attach support struts to the posts on the insides of the row.

Pruning and training

Hybrid berries and blackberries fruit on the previous years' canes, just as raspberries do, so the trained branches will be fruiting as the new canes develop. Keep things simple. Plant one or two plants of similar types together at the centre of the space available, and tie one or two canes along each wire in both directions. Encourage the new canes to grow up through the centre, which can be kept clear for this purpose. Once the plants are established, the canes that have fruited are cut out, allowing the new canes to be tied in.

Increasing your stock

Hybrids and cultivated blackberries reproduce by tip rooting, just as wild blackberries do. If the end of a branch touches the ground it will naturally start to develop roots. If your plants are healthy, encourage this tendency by burying the end of a branch in the soil. In a few months' time, it will have rooted and can then be severed from the parent plant and transplanted to a new site.

Harvesting

These berries are harvested with their plug. Their use and storage needs are similar to those for raspberries (see page 83).

Feeding

Top dress your plants once every two to three years at the same rate as for raspberries (see page 82). Whereas raspberries are fed every year, hybrids will need feeding less often.

Blackcurrants

Blackcurrants are packed with Vitamin C and are not difficult to grow. Although they will tolerate some shade, they prefer full sun.

Planting

Blackcurrants are grown as multi-stemmed bushes. Plant them an inch or so lower than the soil mark which shows where they were planted in the nursery. This encourages them to develop a 'stool' – a number of shoots growing directly out of the soil. The bushes should be spaced 1.2–1.5 m (4–5 ft) apart, depending on the variety. Cut back all the shoots to ground level.

Pruning

During the first year, allow the plant to grow freely; it should develop a cluster of five or more shoots. During the second summer, these shoots should provide a small harvest. In the winter of the second year, if the bush is beginning to look overcrowded, cut a third of the fruited wood out. Remove any branches that are touching the ground.

During following winters, remove any weak or diseased shoots, and remove one-third of the older wood, which will be nearly black, down to the stems, concentrating on branches that have the least healthy young shoots.

The 'destructive' method of pruning involves growing blackcurrants in groups of three. This will suit people with big gardens and plenty of space. Each year one of the bushes in the group is pruned to the ground.

Once the rotation is in full swing you will have one bush out of the three growing new wood while the other two are cropped. The method is said to reduce the build-up of disease.

Neglected old bushes may be pruned hard, removing most of the older wood but, before trying to revive them, check they are free of pests and diseases. New bushes are not expensive so don't be afraid to make a clean start.

Harvesting

All the currants grow in bunches like grapes and they are generally eaten cooked. Pick the bunches and lay them carefully in a container. Use them immediately or store in the fridge for a day. Prepare them for cooking by stripping the berries from the stalk with the tines of a dessert fork. If you are using them in purées or jellies, cook them complete with stalks, sieving afterwards.

Increasing your stock

It's possible to take cuttings, but you must make sure that the parent plants are healthy. Follow the method recommended for red and white currants (see page 86).

Feeding

Blackcurrants are greedy feeders. Feed them every spring with compost or manure.

Red and white currants

Although they are closely related to blackcurrants, red and white currants are less prone to disease and have different pruning and feeding needs. They can be grown as bushes, fans or cordons and tolerate a north-facing site.

Growing methods

Bushes are the most straightforward growing method, but, if space is limited, train your plants as cordons or fans so you can grow fruit on north- or east-facing walls and fences.

A cordon currant can have single, double, triple or even quadruple upright branches, growing from a single main stem 10–15 cm (4–6 in) long. Its side branches are carefully controlled and kept to a maximum of 15 cm (6 in) long. If you are very short of space, the cordon training method is better than the fan. You can grow four different varieties, trained as single cordons, in the space taken up by one fan. This could give you a longer cropping season if you choose the varieties carefully.

Planting

Plant bushes at the same level as they were growing in the nursery, about 1.2–1.5 m (4–5 ft) apart, in soil which has been enriched with garden compost or manure. Cordons should be planted 40–45 cm (15–18 in) apart, and fans will require a spread of about 2 m (6 ft).

Support

Bushes need no support, but cordons and fans will need a post and wire system, with wires at 25 cm (10 in) intervals.

Pruning

Prune from late January to early March, but any time between leaf fall and bud burst is acceptable. If grown as bushes, keep the centres of the bushes open and remove any crossing, weak or dying branches. Shorten the branches by about a third in the winter. Trained forms need specialized pruning. It is not difficult but refer to a pruning manual or attend a course.

Feeding

Red and white currants like fertile moisture-retentive soil. They need feeding with manure or garden compost once every three years.

Increasing your stock

Because they are less prone to disease, you can increase your stock by taking hardwood cuttings at pruning time. Choose healthy young shoots 30 cm (1 ft) long and plant them 15 cm (6 in) deep and 15 cm (6 in) apart in a trench. By the following autumn they should be well rooted and ready to plant out.

If you do not have a suitable space in the garden, plant in large pots, five or so to a pot, in a mixture of 50:50 grit and compost. Keep them well watered. They should root in two to three months and can then be potted up in individual pots in a soil-based compost.

Gooseberries

Gooseberries, like red and white currants, do not mind growing in cool and shady positions. There are many varieties to choose from, but try to pick one that is resistant to American Gooseberry Mildew.

Planting

When you are planting gooseberries, you should follow the method that is used for red and white currants (see opposite). You will need plenty of space around each gooseberry bush, and you should allow about 1.5 m (3 ft 6 in).

Pruning

If left to their own devices, gooseberries will develop as a multi-stemmed bush which grows directly from the ground. However, it is generally best to give them a little training as they are notoriously thorny. Growing them on a 'leg', or a single stem, will give ground clearance for the lower branches.

Bare-rooted plants are generally supplied as a single stem with branches. You can create a leg of about 15 cm (6 in) above the soil by rubbing out the lower buds on the main stem and then trimming off any low shoots.

Pruning time is the same as for currants (late January to early March). You should aim to establish a goblet-shaped bush with plenty of space in the centre. This will allow for air circulation, discourage any pests and diseases and also make the job of picking the fruit easier for you. Note that gooseberries can also be grown as cordons or fans in the same way as currants (see opposite).

Standard gooseberries

Standard gooseberries have been grafted onto a special rootstock and their fruiting branches will start 1–2 m (3–4 ft) above the ground. A standard bush will need to be permanently staked and tied. It is pruned in the same way as a normal bush, but it is essential to keep the main stem free of buds.

Harvesting

Always wear gloves to protect your hands and strip the berries from the bush. Gooseberries for cooking should be harvested when they are green, before they are fully mature, but dessert gooseberries should be left to ripen fully. Green gooseberries will keep in a fridge for several days. If you are not going to use them in puréed form, they will need topping and tailing – nip off the stalks and calyxes with your nails or a pair of small scissors.

Increasing your stock

Gooseberries root fairly easily from hardwood cuttings. Follow the instructions for red and white currants (see opposite).

Feeding

Follow the instructions for red and white currants – feed once every three years.

Strawberries

Strawberries like full sun and acid soil, but they will tolerate a wide range of conditions. They can be in season for six weeks from about mid June; you can choose from early, mid-season and late varieties.

Varieties

Cambridge Favourite is a long-standing reliable variety that does well in organic conditions, but there are lots to choose from. You could also extend the season by growing plants in pots in a greenhouse, in polytunnels or under cloches. Perpetual varieties produce a light crop in late summer and autumn, but their spring flush of flowers must be removed.

Planting

Remember that bare-rooted strawberry plants will need the same treatment as the cane and bush fruits when they arrive (see page 82). It is important to plant the crown, or centre bud, of each plant level with the soil. If it is planted too high or too low, the fruiting and health of the plant will be affected.

A woven plastic mulch can be really useful as a weed supressor. You should cultivate the soil carefully, incorporating some garden compost or well-rotted manure, and then lay the mulch over it, pinning it down with long staples made of bent wire. Make holes in the mulch at 30–45 cm (12–18 in) intervals, and plant the plants through it. The mulch keeps the ground weed-free, but the planting hole itself may become weedy and should be checked throughout the year.

Maintenance

Do not allow strawberries to fruit in their first season – remove any flowers, however tempting. If you are really impatient, set aside one or two plants to provide an instant harvest.

If your strawberries are in flower early and a frost threatens, consider protecting them with a length of agricultural fleece at night. Frosted flowers, which have a black eye, or centre, will not produce any fruit.

You can use straw instead of plastic mulch. Tuck it in carefully around the plants just after the first fruits have formed. It was once traditional to set fire to a straw mulch, plants and all, after cropping. However, this is not advisable; remove the straw and compost it.

After fruiting, unless you intend to increase your plant stock, remove any runners – the long stems with baby plants attached – and cut off all the foliage to encourage healthy growth and remove early spots of disease.

Harvesting

Strawberries are best picked with their stalk and calyx. Cup the fruit lightly in your hand, nip off the stem and lay the fruit gently in a bowl. Strawberries vary in colour according to variety so let your nose and sense of taste be your guide. Fruit should be used immediately.

Increasing your stock

Only save runners if you are certain that the parent plant is healthy. Some varieties produce scores whereas others are less prolific. You may find that they have already developed small roots, or incipient roots. Plant in pots or boxes of potting compost, and keep well watered.

A strawberry bed has a life of up to five or six years. After this the plants produce smaller fruit and become less thrifty. You should not replant in the same spot although you can rotate strawberries in a plot, producing fresh plants from runners each year. This avoids the danger of building up pests and diseases, and there is less weeding to do.

Feeding

Strawberries do not need a lot of feeding, which is just as well if you are growing them under a permanent plastic mulch because they will be almost impossible to feed. If weeds have crept into the planting places, you may need to lift the mulch, weed the offending area and then re-lay it. At this point you can add some compost or manure.

If you are using a straw mulch, feed after you have removed it by top dressing lightly with some well-rotted manure or compost if you think that it's necessary.

Grow bags and pots

If you are really short of space, you could try using organic growing bags or large pots. If you have a back problem, you can place them on a raised surface.

Rhubarb

Although most people tend to think of rhubarb as a fruit it is technically a vegetable, as it is the stalk that is edible. Rhubarb is extremely good tempered and very undemanding, although, like everything else in your garden, it will benefit from your care and attention.

Varieties

There is much more to rhubarb than you might think. Harlow Carr Royal Horticultural Society Gardens holds the National Rhubarb Collection with a staggering 130 varieties, but you will have only a limited number from which to choose. Timperley Early lives up to its name and can be forced (see Harvesting). Champagne is another early variety, with very pale pink stems. Victoria is an old favourite and is extremely reliable.

Planting rhubarb

Rhubarb crowns or sets are available in winter. Rhubarb that is thriving makes huge clumps and occasionally it will need to be lifted and divided, so if you have a friend with a large, healthy clump, ask if they will provide you with some chunks of crown.

Rhubarb is often a Cinderella in the vegetable garden, and you should plant it in some rich soil with added compost for the best results. Remember to water your rhubarb if the summer months are dry, especially during its first year. Your plants will also appreciate a feed with manure or compost each spring. Fortunately, rhubarb is almost immune to most pests and diseases.

Harvesting

Do not be tempted to harvest any of the stems during the first year – the plant needs to establish itself. The following year, you can harvest the stems lightly, but you should not expect a bumper crop until another year has passed. You can start pulling the stems as soon as they appear, and should stop in July. This is partly to give the plant the chance to rest, and partly because rhubarb tends to become tougher after this. You can harvest strawberry rhubarb until September.

Forced rhubarb

Rhubarb can also be forced – brought into bearing early in the year several weeks before it would naturally be ready to harvest. You can do this by digging up a crown in December or January, and then keeping it away from the light in a dark shed or a greenhouse.

Alternatively, you can cover the plants when they appear through the soil with a large bucket and remove it when they start growing in earnest. Forced rhubarb cooks to a stunning shocking pink, and has a delicate flavour. It is one of the great culinary pleasures of early spring and is excellent made into crumbles and pies and mixed into custards.

Fruit trees

Horticulturalists call tree fruit 'top fruit' – for obvious reasons. Soft fruit will give you a harvest within a year, but apples, pears, plums and cherries, along with the more unusual quince and medlar, are a long-term proposition. They will take three years or more to fruit in most cases.

If you have moved to a garden that already has old fruit trees, you should give them at least two seasons if you want to truly test their productivity. Some apple varieties tend to crop every other year (biennially).

A large, old tree adds a great deal visually to a garden or hedgerow, even if, or perhaps especially if, it's gnarled and twisted, so let it stay if you like it. If it has survived this long without attention and is obviously fairly happy, it probably will not need much pruning, apart from removing dead, diseased and dying wood.

Try and get its fruit identified – someone who lives nearby may know exactly what you have. Apples and pears can often be identified at an Apple Day. An apple that does not taste good in October may store well. It might be an old cider apple, possibly a local variety that is now hard to find.

Choosing fruit trees

This can be a complex business but learning about them can be very rewarding. Garden centres will stock the standard varieties of bare-rooted trees in December and January and container-grown trees all the year round. Choosing from their selection will be safe and easy, but it can also be very rewarding to carry out your own research, especially if you are making a considerable investment.

Apart from disease resistance, you will want to consider the flavour and appearance of the crop. With top fruit, you must also consider the final size that you want the tree to be and how it will be pollinated.

Size depends on the roots

If you are planting top fruit for the first time, take a long, hard look at your garden and decide what you have room for. Fruit trees are rarely planted on their own roots these days. Instead, the variety is grafted onto another tree – a rootstock whose function is to influence the final size of the tree. Rootstocks for trees come in a variety of forms.

Apples

For apple trees, MM106 is a good standard rootstock which will produce a tree of about 4–5 m (13–16 ft) which will not object to poor soil. M26 will produce a slightly smaller tree, about 3–5 m (10–15 ft), which will perform well on light soils. Some dwarfing rootstocks, M9 – 1.8–3 m (6–10 ft) – and M27 – 1.5–1.8 m (4–6 ft) – are also available, but they will need permanent staking.

Pears, plums and cherries

There is also a choice of rootstocks for these trees. Pears come on two main rootstocks. Quince C produces a tree of 2.4–3 m (8–10 ft) while Quince A is larger: 3.6–4.5 m (12–13 ft). Plums do not usually make very large trees if they are grown on the standard St Julian A rootstock, with a maximum height of about 3 m (10 ft). It is also possible to grow dwarf plums on the Pixy rootstock which will reach no more than 2.5 m (8 ft).

Cherries are usually grown on the Colt rootstock which results in a small- to medium-sized tree. Other rootstocks introduced over the past few years are Hexaploid Colt, which produces a smaller tree, and Gisela 5, a truly dwarfing rootstock which reaches a maximum of 2.5 m (8 ft).

Trained forms

If you do not have enough space for a normal-sized tree, then you could try a trained form. Apples, plums and pears can all be grown as cordons, espaliers and fans.

Cordons

These are single-stemmed trees which are usually grown at an angle of 45–60 degrees and are perhaps the easiest trained trees to manage. They take up little space in your garden and thus will allow you to produce small quantities of several varieties.

Espaliers and fans

These have pairs of branches trained at regular intervals and at right angles to the main trunk. Fan-trained trees are another possibility for all the main forms of top fruit. Such trees take on a 'flat' two-dimensional form and can make a pleasant and productive screen in the garden, or will grow against a wall or fence.

You can buy ready-trained espaliers and fans at an extra cost, or you can train them yourself. However, do not forget to take pollination into account (see below).

Stepover and ballerina trees

For apples, there's also the option of growing stepover trees – low-growing, single-layered espaliers which can be used at the edge of a border – or 'ballerina' trees, which grow upright on a single stem with no main branches.

Pollination

Fruit will not develop unless its blossoms are pollinated. This means that unless you choose a self-fertile variety you will need to consider planting more than one tree when you are choosing apples, pears, plums or cherries. Each variety belongs to a flowering group and possesses a number or letter which relates to the time when the tree is in blossom.

Most catalogues or specialist fruit books list varieties and their flowering groups in table form. As long as you choose your fruit trees from the same flowering group, or the one above or below it, then pollination should not be a problem for you. Triploid apples need two other trees nearby. If you live in an area where there are fruit trees in nearby gardens, then you will get a boost from the pollinating power of their trees.

Self-fertile varieties will yield satisfactorily without a pollinator, although all fruit produces more heavily if there are pollinators nearby. Your apples could be helped if you plant a crab apple to act as a universal pollinator. It will also make an attractive feature in the garden.

Planting fruit trees

The following instructions apply to all top fruit trees. The greatest choice of varieties is available if you buy bare-rooted trees. Like bare-rooted soft fruit plants, these are despatched during the winter.

● If you receive your bare-rooted tree during a frosty period, leave it wrapped for a day or two. When the weather is mild, unwrap the tree and soak the roots overnight in a bucket of water. If you are not ready to plant the tree, just heel the roots in (see page 80).

● When you are ready to plant, make sure you have a short post and a soft tree tie handy. Lay a plastic sheet, or a split-open black bin liner next to the place you want to plant your tree. Carefully remove the turf and stack separately on the sheet before removing the topsoil and stacking it separately on the sheet. Finally, dig the hole at least 1 m (3 ft) in diameter, or twice that on heavy soils, and slightly deeper than the required depth. Put the subsoil also on the sheet in its own pile.

● To begin with, your tree may need staking on the side from which the prevailing wind comes to give it a firm anchorage in its first year or so. Hammer a 1 m (3 ft) stake into the hole before you plant the tree – away from the hole's centre. Chop up the turf and put it back in the hole, where it will break down and supply your tree with nutrients. At this point, you can also add a bucket of well-rotted manure or compost.

● Place your tree in the hole – it helps to have an assistant to keep it upright – and then gently put some soil around its roots, starting with the topsoil, which has the most nutrients. You will need to plant the tree at the same depth at which it was planted in the nursery – look for the soil mark on the main stem to determine this.

● Gently move the tree up and down initially to make sure that the soil fills in all the gaps around the roots. Keep on filling, making sure that there are no air spaces, until the soil reaches the level of the surrounding area. Firm gently with your foot, and add a little more soil if necessary. Attach the tree to the stake.

Container-grown trees

You can plant container-grown trees at any time of year, leaving the rootball intact, and finishing with the level of the top of the pot at the same level as the soil in the garden.

Protecting fruit trees

If you have problems with rabbits in your garden, or if your cat tends to scratch small tree trunks, you should use a guard around the young fruit tree – either a spiral one, which will expand as the tree grows, or a 'green house' type.

You will also need to check that your tree is still firmly in place once every month or so throughout the winter and spring. If there is an air space between the soil and the trunk, then firm it with your foot.

Keep a circle of at least 1 m (3 ft) of soil free of weeds around young trees to prevent the weeds taking over and robbing them of food. Young trees will need plenty of water during their first year while they are still establishing their root system – at least two large bucketfuls every week in summer if the weather is dry. Do not let any tree set fruit in its first year; it needs to establish itself. It could carry a small harvest in the second year.

Pruning fruit trees

There are some general principles for pruning fruit trees although different varieties have special requirements. Even if all you are trying to do is to reduce the size of a tree, do not attempt to do it without looking at a specialist book or taking expert advice first.

The main rules that apply to pruning all standard trees are to remove any crossing, dead, diseased and dying wood, and to keep the centre of the tree open.

If you have a very vigorous standard tree and need to reduce its size, beware! Pruning can stimulate a lot of long, whippy, non-productive growth, which is known as 'water wood' or water shoots. Try to prune in July when the sap is at its highest. You will lose some fruit, unfortunately, but the growth during the following year will be less vigorous.

An old unproductive apple tree can be renovated. This is best done over a couple of seasons. Refer to a good book or, better still, try and find an expert to help you do this.

You should not be afraid of pruning slowly, especially if the tree is quite large. Just take your time and walk round the tree frequently, observing it carefully to get a good idea of how the shape is looking.

General pruning rules

- Never prune plums or cherries in the winter as you will be putting them at risk of contracting silver leaf disease. They need little pruning on the whole, and it should be done between April and the end of August.
- Apples and pears are best pruned in the dormant season when the tree has no leaves and its shape is easy to see.
- Trained forms will need winter and summer pruning, and you should study a pruning manual carefully, especially if you have paid for a pre-trained espalier or fan.

Apples

There is a huge number of apple varieties, both for dessert and cooking. Remember to look for disease resistance, find out your local varieties and make sure that the trees are from compatible flowering groups.

Varieties

It is perfectly possible to eat a home-grown apple every week from August right through until the following April by choosing varieties that mature at different times. For example, the season could start with Beauty of Bath, Vistabella and Discovery and finish with Tydeman's Late Orange or D'Arcy Spice.

You cannot beat a Bramley for cooking, although there are many culinary varieties to choose from. Eating apples are a personal matter, and everyone will have their favourites.

Feeding

Larger apple trees will not need much feeding. Those on M26 will need feeding once every three years, while the more dwarfing M9 and M27 may need feeding more frequently.

Thinning

Apples will jog along quite nicely on their own, but they sometimes overdo things and will become very heavily laden. For the sake of the tree, and to get the best-quality fruit, it is advisable to thin, especially if you are growing trained forms. This means removing the young fruits so that they are at 10–15 cm (4–6 in) intervals. Start this operation about six weeks after blossoming has finished.

Harvesting

Be aware when your fruit is likely to be ready to harvest. As the time draws near, visit the trees at least once a week. In a particularly hot or dry summer, fruit may ripen two or three weeks earlier than normal. If you miss the ripening time, the ground beneath your tree will be littered with windfalls which won't keep.

Cup your hand under one of the apples and lift it gently on its stalk. If it is ripe, it will leave the tree easily. Don't put any pressure on the fruit itself and place it gently in a container. Rough handling will result in bruising which may not even be visible at harvest time but which will reduce the storage life of your fruit.

Storing the fruit

Lay the fruit on trays in a cool but frost-free place, preferably in the dark. Around 7°C (46°F) is the ideal temperature. The apples should not touch and can be wrapped individually in paper. Small quantities can be put into plastic food bags. Tie at the top and make an air hole with a pencil. Use larger apples first as they tend not to keep as well as medium-sized ones.

Inspect the stored fruit regularly – one bad apple can infect the rest and rots will spread from apple to apple, so the sooner a bad one is removed the better.

Pears

The requirements for growing pears are similar to those for apples, but they will generally need a slightly warmer site. Pear trees are ideal for smaller gardens as they respond well to training and can be grown successfully against a warm wall as an espalier.

Maintenance

The planting, pruning and feeding instructions for pear trees are the same as those that are given for apples (see page 97). Remember that pear trees also need pollinators.

Harvesting

Apart from the earliest varieties, pears need to ripen off the tree so keep an eye on them as harvesting time approaches. Pick them as soon as they will part company from the branch when they are lifted in the palm of your hand at a slight angle. Like apples, they should be handled with care like eggs from the moment they are picked to avoid any bruising.

Very late ripening pears, such as Glou Morceau and Josephine de Malines, which need the sunniest growing situation, can be left on the tree until the first ones fall, and should then be harvested straight away. Most will keep until January, but the cooking pear Catillac should keep until the early spring.

Storing pears

Once picked, pears can be stored at cooler temperatures than apples – ideally, 0–1°C (32–34°F). Do not wrap them. However, it is difficult to keep them this cool in the average home. They need to be watched carefully as it is only a short step from a perfectly ripe pear to an over-ripe 'sleepy' one. If your crop is small and you have only a few pears, you could even store them at the bottom of the fridge in a plastic bag.

Quinces and medlars

These are more unusual fruit but well worth growing. Quinces can be added to apples and pears in pies and crumbles or made, like medlars, into a delicious paste or amber-coloured jelly.

Quinces

The quince is a delightful tree – it is airy in structure with striking blossom. As well as being self fertile, it does not need pruning, apart from the common-sense removal of congested, dead, diseased or dying wood. Nor does it need feeding. Quinces are not too particular about soil, but they do better in milder areas. The fruits are aromatic, and make a wonderful glowing red jelly. They are also very hard, so can't be eaten raw. Jane Grigson recommended putting a few slices of quince in an apple pie to transform its flavour.

You may have come across the ornamental Japanese quince, commonly known as Japonica (chaenomeles). Its fruits are edible, but they are poor relations of the true quince, which has large rounded golden fruits covered in a light down.

Quinces have no special requirements as far as planting is concerned – you should just follow the instructions on page 95. Their one main problem is quince leaf blotch, which is disfiguring, but not deadly. The variety Krymsk is said to be less susceptible to this.

Medlars

The medlar is not commonly grown nowadays. Its fruits are small and brownish, with a large open calyx. The medlar fruit has to be 'bletted', i.e. almost rotted, until it is soft and brown before harvesting and cooking. It makes a jelly which is good with game.

It is also an ornamental and relatively easy tree to grow, and needs no feeding and little pruning. It will need staking for the first few years as it tends to be top heavy as a youngster.

Plums

The plum harvest starts at the end of July with Early Rivers, and finishes at the end of September with Marjorie's seedling. In between are some of the most delectable fruits imaginable, which are far superior to any imported plum that you can buy.

Varieties

There are so many varieties of plum, but one of the most popular is the Victoria, not least because it is self fertile, so if you can only have one plum tree in your garden, a Victoria could be for you. Connoisseurs can be a bit sniffy about its flavour, but most people love it. Although it is thought of as a dessert plum it cooks well and makes delicious jam.

The Warwickshire Drooper is the true cottager's plum. It grows on its own roots, so you can produce your own trees from any suckers that grow. It is hardy and largely disease free, and is an excellent cooking plum. It is also good eaten raw, especially if you can reach the fruit at the very top of the tree, when it is slightly flushed with red.

Damsons

The deep purple damson, with its grape-like bloom, is a form of plum. It is often not very pleasant to eat raw, but bursts with flavour when it is cooked. Damsons are usually tough and undemanding to grow. Together with Droopers, they are traditionally planted within the hedge line, and this can be a space-saving way of increasing the fruit in your garden if you have a suitable boundary.

Gages

For flavour, most people would recommend the gages. A warm, ripe greengage is a delicious treat. Although they may fruit less reliably in cooler areas, it is always well worth the wait for a good year with a sizeable crop. Popular gages include Ouillins Golden Gage and Coe's Gold Drop.

Pruning

Plums should only be pruned when they are in active growth during the period from May to early September. If they are pruned in winter, their open wounds will be susceptible to infection by silver leaf, a fungal disease which renders the trees unproductive.

They generally prefer not to be pruned at all, so you should only take off the dead, diseased and dying wood, together with any crossing branches that you think may be affecting the shape and growth of the tree.

Pollination

Plums, like all the other top fruit, need to be chosen with pollination in mind, so be sure to check whether your tree is self-fertile, or needs a pollination companion.

Cherries

Cherries are not the easiest of fruit to grow but the rewards are wonderful if you are prepared to be patient and do not expect a bumper harvest every year. They thrive in mild areas but can also be grown successfully against a warm wall in colder areas.

Varieties

Stella is a popular self-fertile variety, which is ideal if you only want one tree. The fruit is a deep ruby red, but beware – the birds will eat them when they are at the pink and yellow stage of early ripening.

Growing any variety of dessert cherry is usually a race against the birds. Commercial cherries are low growing and are planted in fruit cages. In gardens, fan training can be the answer, as the cherry tree can easily be protected with netting. There are many varieties available, so browse through a specialist catalogue if you intend to plant several.

Acid or Morello cherries are self fertile, tolerate lower temperatures, and can be grown successfully against a north-facing wall.

Pruning

Like plums, cherries are prone to silver leaf disease and should only be pruned when they are in active growth. Acid cherries have a different growth habit, and fruit on the previous season's wood. Remove a few of the older branches in a rotation system after three or four years.

Harvesting

Pick dessert cherries by the stalk, not the fruit, as soon as they are ripe – you may have to discipline yourself to wait that long. They need to be eaten quickly as they will not store for more than a day or two in the fridge, but they can be made into jam, bottled or frozen.

Morello-type cherries need to be harvested by cutting the stalks from the tree with scissors. Their distinctive sour flavour makes them ideal for bottling, making into jam and compôtes, preserving in alcohol, or cooking in classic dessert dishes, such as clafoutis.

Pest and disease control

Commercially-grown, non-organic fruit trees are often sprayed but organic fruit in a smallholding or garden probably won't be sprayed at all. Growing fruit on a smaller scale reduces the risk of pests and diseases.

Varieties and habitat

By choosing resistant varieties, you can help avoid many pests and diseases. Look at local varieties which are well adapted for your soil and climate and likely to yield well. Make sure the habitat near the trees encourages predatory insects, such as lacewings or hoverflies, whose young devour aphids. However, if you have no aphids at all, the predators will die out, so aim for a balance. Encourage beneficial creatures by growing open-faced and composite flowering plants, like limnanthes, convolvulus tricolor, calendula and phacelia, near the fruit.

Where there are aphids, you may also see ants. Ants 'farm' aphids, moving them around to choice feeding sites on your tree – the most succulent growing shoots – and 'milking' them of the honeydew they produce. A grease band or smear of petroleum jelly round the base of the tree prevents ants from climbing the trunk.

Garden hygiene

Simple hygiene measures will protect against disease. You should clear up fallen leaves and fruits under trees and bushes, and remove any shrivelled 'mummified' fruits. In the past, the best way to deal with diseased plant material was to burn it, but now you have other options. Bag the material up immediately to contain the disease spores, and take it to your nearest civic amenity site where there is usually a green waste recycling area. If you have a green waste home collection scheme, put the waste straight in the bin. Disinfect tools after using them.

Inspect your plants

Stressed plants are the most likely ones to succumb to disease. If they are too dry, too crowded, overfed or starved, pests and diseases will target them. To nip problems in the bud, you need to know your plants well, looking at them several times a week and noting any unusual symptoms. If you spot a problem early enough, simply rub out pest insects with your finger and thumb, or cut out diseased shoots. Mulching can also help.

Virus diseases

All plants can suffer from these, which can be transmitted by aphids. Plants fail to thrive and may have discoloured leaves. You need to make a positive diagnosis as viral symptoms can be confused with mineral deficiencies. There is usually no remedy so buy plants from a source that guarantees virus-free stock. Keep them growing healthily and do not overfeed them. If virus strikes, dig up the affected plants and burn them before finding a new growing area.

Pests and diseases

Name	Symptom	Treatment
American gooseberry mildew	This disease also affects blackcurrants and, occasionally, red and white currants. It first appears on new shoots as a white powdery patch, and eventually covers berries with a felt-like mould.	Make sure there is plenty of space around the plants and that they are carefully pruned with an open centre to allow air to circulate. Dispose of any prunings hygienically. Plant in open, sunny situations. The best defence is to use resistant varieties.
Apple powdery mildew	This can affect pears, too, but usually not severely. Apple powdery mildew can reduce yields and affect the vigour of the tree. It appears in spring as a white powdery coating on leaves and shoots, and may also affect blossom, which withers and drops. It overwinters in buds, and spreads most quickly in summer when nights are humid. A harsh winter cuts down infection.	Cut out the affected wood several centimetres below the site of the infection and dispose of the prunings hygienically. Buds will be distorted, and shoots a silvery grey. Carry on doing this throughout the season. The best defence is to choose varieties that have some resistance to mildew, such as Discovery, D'Arcy Spice and Worcester Pearmain.
Apple scab	This affects apples and pears. Some varieties of apple are very prone to scab, which is also more prevalent in cool, wet areas of the country. It is a fungal disease which produces brown patches on the leaves. It may spread to fruits, which will have corky patches which sometimes crack, although the fruit does not rot.	The fungus overwinters on fallen leaves, so clear these up as soon as you can, or run the lawnmower over them so that they break down as quickly as possible. You could also water the area with diluted urine to help speed up breakdown. Twigs can be affected, and the patches may swell and burst. Try to choose resistant varieties.
Apple sawfly	Apple sawfly eggs are laid on blossom and embryo fruit in spring. Fruit falls from the tree early, and there may be a hole in it. The tunnel is filled with brown frass (sawfly larva 'pooh'). Cocoons survive in the ground over winter.	Compost fallen fruit. Cultivate the ground around the tree if sawfly has been a problem so that the cocoons are exposed for predators.
Bacterial canker	This disease affects plums and cherries. Brown spots appear on the leaves late in spring, and these eventually become holes. Gum may start leaking from the branches or trunk, and leaves and stems may die back. Plums Marjorie's Seedling and Warwickshire Drooper are said to have some resistance.	Prune out affected branches in summer, well below the infection, and dispose of the prunings hygienically. Take great care not to wound tree trunks or branches.
Blackcurrant big bud	The buds swell and become noticeably larger than normal buds. This is because they are harbouring the blackcurrant gall mite. This can happen at any time of year.	Limit the infection by picking the enlarged buds off by hand, especially in winter and early spring, and disposing of them hygienically. Remove heavily infected plants. The mite is thought to spread reversion virus.

Name	Symptom	Treatment
Blackcurrant leaf spot	Small brown spots appear on the leaves and gradually join up. The leaves may turn yellow and fall early. The fruit may shrivel, and bushes can weaken.	Pick off any diseased leaves, remove all fallen leaves and burn them; remove any branches that touch the soil.
Blackcurrant reversion virus	This is quite hard to spot, but the leaves generally look different from normal growth, and the yield declines even though the bush is growing well. You may need an expert diagnosis, as the symptoms are hard to recognize.	There is no cure: the affected bushes must be removed and burnt.
Brown rot	This affects apples, pears, plums and cherries. Fruits rot on the tree, with brown patches, often covered in powdery-looking white spots.	Remove fallen fruit, and any mummified fruit that is still hanging on the tree.
Brown rot in plums	This causes blossoms to wilt and twigs to die back, so prune out the affected branches. At fruiting time, rotting plums will hang on the branches, turning brown with white spots or rings. Remove them, along with any mummified fruits.	Pick up fallen fruit and remove any fruit that is hanging on at the end of the season. These are often affected by diseases and will spread the spores if they are not removed. Dispose of them hygienically.
Cane blight	This affects raspberries, hybrid berries and strawberries. The leaves shrivel and die, dark patches and cracked bark develop on the canes and become covered with pustules.	Disease enters through wounds, so always handle the canes carefully. Cut out any diseased canes below ground level. Disinfect your tools afterwards.
Canker	This affects apples and pears. Canker enters the tree through a wound, so an area where a scab has caused a twig to burst may provide an entry point for the disease. Twigs and branches die back, and there may be swelling or deep cracks.	Prune out the affected branches well below the diseased portion, which shows as a discoloured area, and dispose of them hygienically. The fruit may crack and remain mummified on the tree, so remove any mummified fruit. The disease is spread when spores are splashed onto branches by wind and rain. You can minimize this by allowing grass to grow up to the tree once it is established.
Codling moth	This affects apples and pears. Codling moths may enter through the fruit's calyx but its exit will result in a hole in your otherwise perfect apple.	Put up pheromone traps in mid-May. These little roofed platforms conceal a pheromone which smells like a female moth but it is concealed under a sticky surface. Male moths attracted to the scent find themselves stuck and perish, reducing overall moth numbers.
Fire blight	This affects pears, turning the flowering shoots brown. Leaves wither and turn dark brown. This is a serious disease.	The affected branches need to be pruned back to around a metre below the end of the branch. It can mean that a small tree has to be destroyed.

Name	Symptom	Treatment
Gooseberry sawfly	Keep a close eye on your plants in late April, late June and late August as the sawfly has several hatchings. The larvae eat the leaves, and can skeletonize a whole bush. Look for them on the undersides of leaves, especially on any with pin-holes, and crush them. After hatching, the pest eats solidly for about three weeks and then drops to the ground and forms cocoons which stay in the soil until the following spring. Removing mulches and then cultivating the soil around the bushes in late autumn and early winter brings the cocoons to the surface where birds – or chickens – will relish them.	It is possible to spray the plants with Derris or pyrethrum, but it is probably not worthwhile, as the sprays are not effective unless they come into contact with the larvae on the undersides of the leaves, and this is difficult to achieve.
Grey mould (Botrytis) in strawberries	Fruits suffer from brownish-grey fluffy mould which can be widespread if the summer is wet.	Pick off the affected fruits and put them in the dustbin.
Iron deficiency in cane fruits	This is sometimes mistaken for virus infection. Yellow blotches appear on the leaves between veins. It often occurs when raspberries are grown on alkaline soil.	Make sure your plant suits the soil type and that the area is well drained. Extra feeding with manure or well-rotted compost may be necessary.
Leaf curling plum aphid	Shoots and young leaves are distorted by this yellow-green aphid. It looks bad, but a healthy tree usually survives and fruits in spite of it.	You should refer to the general instructions on encouraging beneficial insects (see page 102).
Pear leaf blister mite	This is not usually serious, although the affected leaves look unsightly with yellow, red or green blisters on either side. This is where the tiny mites live and breed.	Picking off the leaves when you see them will disrupt the cycle. In severe cases, fruit can be affected and will fall early, but this is not common.
Pear midge	Pear midge damages fruitlets, which turn black and drop off. If an affected fruit is cut open, you will find it is filled with small white caterpillars. If the fruit does not drop, the caterpillars will emerge from cracks in the fruit. They will then form cocoons in the soil ready to infest your tree again the following season.	Mulch beneath the tree with black plastic, carpet or cardboard in March. This prevents the midge emerging from the soil and flying up to lay its eggs on the unopened blossoms. If you see any affected fruit during the summer, especially in June, pick them up, or pick them off the tree and burn them or take them to your municipal waste site.
Plum moth	If you find a wriggling white, pink or red caterpillar in the centre of your plum this is the culprit.	Pheromone traps are available to lure the male plum moth to its death.
Plum sawfly	This is another pest that you will find in the centre of a plum. This time you will see an entry hole with a dark sticky substance oozing from it. Affected fruit falls early.	This problem does not usually happen every year. Collect the fallen fruit, as the caterpillars will crawl out to overwinter in the soil.

Name	Symptom	Treatment
Raspberry beetle	This also affects the hybrid berries. The beetle feeds on the berries and causes parts of them to shrivel.	Fork lightly around the canes during the winter to expose the pupae so that birds can eat them. If you have chickens, let them scratch among the roots. This technique will also help to reduce populations of raspberry moth and cane midge. If you get a severe infestation, consider cutting all the canes to ground level in the autumn, but remember that you may lose your summer fruiting raspberry crop.
Raspberry cane and leaf spot	Attacks all the cane fruits, producing purple spots on canes, leaves, stalks and blossom. The yield of fruit is reduced. A severe case causes the death of infected plants. Cut out diseased canes as soon as you see them and burn them.	You can spray with a Bordeaux mixture, a copper fungicide, as a last resort. Spray when the buds begin to open on fruiting canes. Repeat after 10 days.
Raspberry spur blight	This affects raspberries and loganberries. Brown spots can appear on leaves in early summer, followed by purple spots on the stems near buds, which turn black or silver in winter.	Cut out diseased canes and burn them. Make sure the canes are not overcrowded. Fungal diseases thrive where air circulation round canes is poor. Disease is worse after wet, windy springs. You can use Bordeaux mixture as a last resort. Spray in spring, starting when buds are 1 cm ($1/2$ in long) and then repeating three more times at 14-day intervals.
Strawberry beetle	If seeds are missing from your strawberries, this little brown beetle is the culprit.	It also eats weed seeds, so make sure there are no seeding weeds close by. There is no acceptable organic treatment, but it isn't usually a severe problem.
Winter moths	These affect apples, pears, plums and cherries. The caterpillars eat holes in leaves and may damage blossom.	Use fruit tree bands or grease between October and March to prevent the crawling phase of the winter moth from reaching the branches. You will need to put bands on stakes as well, if you are using them.
Woolly aphid	This affects apples. A woolly aphid colony looks like a pile of white fluff on twigs or branches. This hides and protects the aphids inside. They can cause hard growths or galls on trees, which are not a problem unless they then develop surface fissures which can allow canker to enter the branch.	Scrape off the 'wool' as soon as you see it. If there are any very badly affected branches, prune them out. If there is a very heavy infestation, you should spray with insecticidal soap two or three times, allowing one or two days between treatments.

part 2
home farm

Keeping hens

Keeping a few hens organically in your garden is a fantastic means of gaining delicious fresh eggs. Your garden will be well manured and will flourish and, hopefully, you will thoroughly enjoy the whole experience as you get closer to nature. The simplest system is usually the most successful, and it is easiest to start with just two or three hens and to keep them in a henhouse with a run plus as much access to your garden as you can bear. As partners in your garden, and properly managed, your flock will fulfil many roles and bring you great pleasure as you watch them scratching or indulging in a dust bath.

First steps

Start with a couple of the better-laying pure breeds, or one of the hybrids specially designed for free range. Remember that hens bred for their beauty or size have lost their utility characteristics. The male of the species is not recommended for beginners – you don't need a cock's involvement for your hens to produce eggs.

Keeping hens is not difficult, despite what you may have read. Most fowl problems are caused by stress and over-crowding. So let the size of your garden determine the size of your flock, and remember those at the bottom of the pecking order – smaller flocks make for happier hens.

If you like the idea of keeping hens, then before you rush out and buy some birds there are important decisions to make and practical steps to take. First, you must contact your local Environmental Health Officer to check if there are any contra-indications to poultry keeping in the local by-laws. Next, and most importantly, talk to your neighbours to see if they will help if you are away and will put up with any noise. Hens make little sound that could be considered a nuisance but, sadly, the cock's crow – a cry that must have rung out across the countryside throughout history – is now the subject of conflict on the front page of every local newspaper.

On to expense. Assuming you decide on two or three hens, you can expect to pay only a small amount per week on feed, depending on how big your garden is and how much surplus kitchen and garden waste that your household generates.

Why keep hens?

- They are producers of first-rate eggs (and also home-raised meat by using surplus cockerels, if you want to go down that route).
- In the garden, they supply top-grade organic fertilizer and compost activator, and their bedding makes excellent soil conditioner. Additionally, they can be used as scarifiers, land clearers and even effective pest controllers.
- They can double-up as pets for your children, a hobby for those who want to get involved in the Fancy, and, last but not least, they introduce an element of drama, colour and movement into the garden. A plot without poultry is a drab and lifeless place.

Sourcing hens

Finding your hens gives you the opportunity to make some good contacts. Look locally first, then go to shows (see page 205). Don't buy from markets; no-one sends their best birds to market. The small ads section in the poultry and smallholding press features breeders. If you want to start with organic stock, the Soil Association can help, or you can beg, borrow and barter some hens with a fellow organic henkeeper. Give yourself plenty of time; you may have to order and wait for eggs to hatch and chicks to grow. Most breeders sell spring hatched pullets at 20 weeks old in September. Always visit before buying.

Maintenance and care

Make sure that you have your run, house and food ready and waiting for your new hens before you go and collect them. And, finally, although henkeeping is generally trouble-free, remember that your hens must be visited at least twice a day and cleaned out once a week. It won't take long – just a few minutes a day – but beware, keeping hens could develop into a consuming passion.

Where to keep your flock

First, decide on where to site your run. You should choose a shady, sheltered spot as near to the house as possible. Your hens' main enemies are uncontrolled dogs (your own pets can be trained) and, of course, foxes. If you live in a foxy area, then shelve any henkeeping plans for another time and place; it is not worth the heartbreak or the expense.

The ideal site is sheltered and sunny, providing as much space as you can, especially if you want your flock to spend time there. Allow maximum free range, depending on the vulnerability of your plants and the risk to your hens from predators. Some people let their flock out of the run when they get home from work. The troupe will make their own way back to roost as light fades because they cannot see in the dark and need the security of home. Even if your hens spend most of their time in the garden, you will still need somewhere safe to keep them at night.

Rotating the run

In a fulltime run, it is best to divide the space in two, with the henhouse in the middle and popholes on both sides, so you can move your birds every three months and rest the other half of the run. Short grass is good for hens, so by rotating their quarters you can make sure it is always available. Dig over the run while the hens are in situ; it keeps them busy and the area is ready to re-seed as they move on. Do not use those little arks, even though you can move the run to pastures new each day – they are far too small for anything other than two bantams or a broody and chicks.

Size and security

An adequate chicken run is 8 m (24 ft) square, fenced with 2 m (6 ft) high chicken wire, the bottom 20 cm (8 in) dug into the ground to stop tunnelling predators. It has a self-closing door. The level of security round your run will depend on local predators. Install strong netting and wired roofs. Remove overhanging branches or sheds on the perimeter of the run to keep out foxes, mink, rats, badgers and cats.

You can use sonic devices pitched to deter foxes, but a determined one will put up with any discomfort for a good meal. Site your run as near to your house as you can bear.

Mud and shade

If you have heavy soil your run will get muddy in winter. Cover the floor with dry leaves or straw and position straw bales for shelter from cold winds. Use a wooden pallet as a plinth for feeders and drinkers, and protect the route to your run with a roll up path or permanent paving. Take care not to slip. Shade is as important as shelter; poultry don't thrive in hot weather. Large shrubs and trees, with their roots protected from dust bathers with large flints or stones, are ideal, but bamboo or willow panels will offer temporary shade.

Henhouses

An existing shed can be customized with a pophole and roosting pole provided it is secure, waterproof and draughtproof. Alternatively, you can opt for a ready-made henhouse, but be sceptical about the number of occupants the makers boast it will hold. Space needed per bird for perch, nestbox or pophole is:

- 35 sq cm (15 sq in) per large hen
- 30 sq cm (12 sq in) per medium hen
- 25 sq cm (9 sq in) per bantam.

Hens will all hutch up together to sleep but good ventilation is important. Some hens roost and others do not; it does not matter as long as you change their bedding regularly. You can remove the perches to increase the headroom.

Mount your house on 45 cm (18 in) legs or a plinth with a ramp for the hens. It will be easier on your back as you clean, and the space underneath will provide a dustbath and won't offer places for rats to lurk. Hens love a good dustbath in dry soil. It removes parasites, and

by siting one in the run you may deter them from digging craters in your vegetable garden.

You can have two or three small henhouses so newcomers have their own place, old ladies can be by themselves, layers can choose a quiet spot and the unwell can be isolated. Some houses have integrated nest boxes with outside access, but several moveable 30 cm (1 ft) square plywood boxes filled with straw are preferable. Hens like to lay in dark, secret places.

If you build your own house, use marine ply rather than lapped boards – there is less opportunity for parasites to hide. Onduline is preferable as a roofing material to tarred felt for the same reason. Do not use creosote.

For bedding materials, dust-free chopped straw, shredded cardboard or newspaper are best. Never use hay – it can harbour moulds. Regular mucking out, especially in summer, will keep your flock in good health as the ammonia in the droppings harms birds' lungs.

Cleaning the henhouse

Clean out your henhouse(s) once a week. Wear gloves, sweeping out the debris with a hand brush and using a decorator's scraper for stubborn bits. Cover the floor with sheets of newspaper. Next time you clean, these can be scooped out, and the bedding/droppings can be shaken on to the compost heap and the paper shredded. As carbon-rich waste, the newspaper will layer on the heap between the nitrogen-rich manure and kitchen garden leftovers. Have a real spring clean every three months: disinfect well, blitz with a car hoover and dust for lice with Pyrethrum if necessary.

Which breed?

There are over 100 breeds of chicken, all originating from the Jungle Fowl which still range the forests of Asia. The variety is astounding, but for the beginner a traditional pure breed or hybrid backyard bird is recommended as these are easy to keep, cheap and widely available.

Some breeds are extraordinarily colourful (and expensive) and if, eventually, you progress to a rarer breed you will have the advantage of knowing you are encouraging an endangered species and retaining its valuable characteristics for the general gene pool.

Hens lay gradually less and less as they age, so start with two or three birds. You can always get a few more next year and prolong your egg supply, or maybe hatch out some under a broody. If you obtain your entire flock at the same time, they will all stop and start laying simultaneously and you will end up with six elderly ladies, eating a lot and laying little. If you stagger your purchases or hatchings, as your older hens drop off one end of the perch you can introduce new pullets which will give you a couple of years' constant laying. This generational approach allows you a gentle introduction to the hobby as a novice and lets you change your allegiance to other breeds.

Bantams or full size?

Chickens come in two sizes: bantam or full size. Most breeds are available in both, though some, such as Silkies and Pekins, are just a small breed. Big girls like the Orpingtons are a good choice – they tend to be more docile –

but for a really small garden, a pair of bantams is ideal. You can keep a flock of different-sized birds as bulk is not paramount in the pecking order. Many people's top hens are bantam crosses kept for their broody prowess.

Hybrids

Commercial hybrids are designed for gargantuan egg production or as meat, usually for battery life, although more recently for free range. In both cases, genes are selected for maximum production at the earliest age, so these birds are short-lived, cannot cope with weather or even carry their own weight. Recently a hybrid has been developed without the aggressive gene so she will not peck her millions of neighbours in so-called free range situations.

Here we recommend a selection of breeds for the beginner. Prices vary, but cheapest is not always best. Whatever you choose, go and see them before you buy, checking that they have been well looked after. Friends' unvaccinated hens or recommendations, and small breeders who concentrate on just a couple of breeds are best. Broody-raised chicks are preferable to those hatched in an incubator. In the end, your choice of chickens will be governed by what you want them for – eggs, meat or pets.

Hens for egg production

Birds bred for their egg-laying prowess have been developed over many centuries to produce the best eggs for the kitchen. Here are some of the best and most popular breeds of hens for egg production.

Sussex (GB)

Broad breasted and plump, the Sussex is the oldest utility dual-purpose bird to be developed in Britain. It lays lots of tinted brown eggs for at least five years. Sussex are easy to hatch and rarely go broody. Hardy and disease resistant, they love free ranging – distance no object. They are available in white with black matching cuff and tail feathers, and also in speckled brown, red, silver and white.

Marans (France)

A prolific layer of nice dark brown eggs (and we like a nice brown egg), the Marans has not been overbred so its utility characteristics have been kept for fear of losing the egg's colour. Madame Marans has red eyes, white feet and dark cuckoo plumage, and is elegant in a housewifely way. Imported from France in 1930, Marans are easy, active and prepared to rough it.

Leghorns (Italy)

With a racy streamlined body, the Leghorn comes in 10 colours. Most of the modern breeding has taken place in the United States because they lay white eggs, which Americans prefer. The Leghorn is recognizable by its huge red comb, upright in cocks and tipping saucily to one side on the ladies. Active and sprightly, with long wattles and white earlobes, it is available in exchequer (black and white) silver duckwing and pyle (muliticoloured).

Hens as pets

These breeds are well known for their friendly dispositions, especially if handled as chicks.

Pekins (China)

With their short legs, feathered feet and toes, Pekins look like little tea cosies. They are excellent for beginners and highly recommended for children. Do not expect regular eggs, however, after the first year. In a wide range of shades (useful if you have several children – each one can have a different colour), Pekins are tiny birds under all that feather. They are good for small urban gardens but watch out for prowling neighbourhood cats.

Silkie (China)

These are the best broodies of all on anyone's eggs, especially a Silkie cross. They are available in black, gold, blue, white and partridge. Soft, with really silky, fluffy fur-like feathers, they are charming birds to keep as pets. Though decorative and fragile looking, they are hardy and lay well when not broody. They are susceptible to scaly leg and have five toes.

Big decorative hens

Larger hens are often more relaxed, self-confident and friendly, and make good pets.

Brahma (Asia)

These tall, aristocratic gentle giants of the hen world were known as rich mens' pets because they do not lay much and eat a lot. Friendly and inquisitive, they have feathered legs, pencilled plumage, small peacombs and heavy eyebrows. The cocks are much taller than their wives so the sexes are easy to differentiate as chicks.

Orpington (GB)

The first Orpington was bred in 1886 in Kent. In buff, black, blue and white, they are of stout and matronly mein but surprisingly energetic.

Apart from their blowsy glamour, it is their friendliness that you will come to love. Laying small tinted eggs, they were originally bred for the table. However, eating your Orpington would be like dining on the family Labrador!

Hybrids for free range

These birds have been selectively bred for maximum egg production in a free range or backyard situation.

Black Rock

Prolific layers of tinted eggs, a mix of Rhode Island Reds and Rocks, these dark, shiny ladies do not go broody and keep their mind on their job – to produce several eggs a week for at least five years. They are bright and jolly and a useful backbone to any small flock.

Speckeldy

A cross between a Marans and a Barred Plymouth Rock, this is a busy utility bird which has all the advantages of its parents and lays nice brown eggs. Lively and energetic, these black and white stripy hens are hardy, can cope with the weather, and forage well. They will not go broody.

Feeding your hens

Hens are omnivores and need a basic diet of grain (in the form of organic mixed corn) and protein that you buy from your feed merchant as pellets. These fundamentals are naturally supplemented with insects from the garden, green stuff from the kitchen and grass from their surroundings.

The more free range your hens are, the less food you will have to supply. Water must be available at all times. They also need grit, which they pick up from the soil, to enable them to digest the food in their crop, but you will have to offer this if your hens are confined. Most birds are quite efficient at balancing their own nutritional requirements.

You can get all your supplies from a local feed merchant. Some companies produce antibiotic, additive and GM-free feed. Your merchant will also be able to supply chick crumbs and oystershell for sound eggshells.

Leftovers

It makes sense to use up household leftovers to feed your flock. Keep a bowl next to the sink for plate scrapings (except meat and fish which may attract vermin if not eaten straight away). You'll soon find out what is palatable. Many hens routinely eat moistened brown bread, sunflower hearts and excess rice and pasta for breakfast in their run; then snack on old cheese, overripe grapes, sweetcorn and apples during the day plus anything they can find in the garden; and then mixed corn – a good slow digesting supper – in the run before they go to roost for the night.

Storing food

Special galvanized water and food containers for keeping feed dry can be bought from suppliers, including a useful automatic feeder. Hens are messy eaters so remove any leftover food in the run to avoid attracting unwelcome diners during the night.

To deter vermin, store your sacks of grain and pellets in small galvanized dustbins with metal lids, buying only one sack of each at a time so it is always fresh. In winter, your birds may be short of greenery, so tie a bunch of spinach, kale or cabbage over them in the run. Better still, let them into the vegetable garden to eat anything that has gone to seed.

Confined hens

If your hens free range in a large garden, the food you offer is not a matter of life or death, but if they are confined in a run, they need a mixed diet. Serve organic protein pellets for breakfast with greenery, oystershell and grit; mixed corn for supper. Keep a compost heap in the run, tipping in garden waste for them to sort through. Hens are creatures of habit, disliking changes in routine or diet, so find out from your breeder what they have been eating and introduce new foodstuffs gradually.

Eggs

Which comes first – the chicken or the egg? It should be the hens every time, but if you look after your hens properly, the eggs will follow. An organic egg is the perfect natural food: unrefined, unprocessed and unenriched – the most versatile ingredient in your larder.

A standard hen's egg weighs 65 g (2¹/₂ oz) whereas a bantam's egg is about 40 g (1¹/₂ oz). There is plenty of variation depending on the breed, age and time of year. You may find your pullet's first egg is tiny and that your old ladies lay huge double yolkers. Occasionally you will see a strange-shaped egg or a soft-shelled one. If these persist, it is worth checking your hens' diet and adding extra oystershell.

Eggs can be shades of brown, white or, in the case of Araucanas, pale blue/green. Hens with white earlobes lay white eggs, but most lay lovely pale brown tinted eggs. The colour of the shell makes no difference to the flavour of the egg – that is affected by what your hen eats. The colour of the yolk is determined by the amount of greenery that she consumes. Deprived of protein, hens don't lay; that's why they stop laying during the annual moult – all their protein is used to produce new feathers.

Eggshells are porous so do not store eggs next to strongly-smelling foods. The eggs can be wiped clean with a loofah or scourer which has been dampened in warm water.

Magpies, squirrels, rats and, occasionally, even hens will eat eggs. To stop this, a nestful of ping pong balls will sometimes do the trick, but the best deterrent is prompt collection.

Always date your eggs with a soft pencil, collect them every day and eat them fresh. To find out about selling surplus organic eggs, phone your local DEFRA office (see page 205) for their latest deliberations on the subject.

Top six pure breed layers

Breed	Eggs per annum
Rhode Island Red	260 tinted eggs
Sussex	260 tinted eggs
Fayoumi	250 tinted eggs
Leghorn	240 white eggs
Friesian	230 white eggs
Marans	200 brown eggs

Augmenting your flock

For a continuing supply of eggs, you should increase your flock by a couple of hens every year or so. Hatching out your own chicks is the most natural way to build up stock. If you do not have a cock or want to try a new breed, you can buy organic fertile eggs from a breeder and hatch them out in an incubator or, best of all, under a broody hen.

If you want chicks

You may have noticed that one of your hens is reluctant to leave the nest box, fluffing up angrily if you disturb her. If you do not want her to sit, remove any eggs she lays and keep shutting her out of the nest box. However, you want chicks, leave her to settle for a couple of days and then move her quietly one evening to a strong cardboard box with a pophole, or to a broody coop in a run in a secluded spot away from the flock. Place the eggs under her, but only increase your flock by two or three at a time. Every day at the same time, gently take her out and make sure she eats, drinks and performs her ablutions.

Looking after chicks

Hatching day is 21 days from the time the hen started sitting. When they hatch, the chicks will stay under their mother for 48 hours. As they appear, offer them some coccidiostat and antibiotic-free chick crumbs sprinkled on the ground and some water in a chick drinker. Remove any unhatched eggs. Mum will show them what to do and keep them warm and safe; your role is supervisory. Keep an eye on the other hens, and don't let them into the coop.

Feed your babes on what the rest of the flock eats, ground up in an old coffee grinder, little and often, and move their run on short grass every day. They will pick up all your flock's immunities and grow up as healthy, vigorous birds.

These newcomers are introduced to the rest of your flock gradually as they grow and can be released from the coop into the run with their mum at four weeks of age. Chicks can be brought in at about twelve weeks but, without a minder, they must be raised in a separate run until they can hold their own.

Alternatively, you can buy pullets at point of lay (20–24 weeks). Whatever aged birds you bring in, they must spend several days cooped up separately inside the run so the other occupants get used to them. It is kinder to buy in pairs rather than singly. It can take ages for a new bird to be accepted into the pecking order, but with lots of space and things to do, it should be a problem only at mealtimes. Let newcomers dine alone for a while.

When you collect your new birds or take them to the vet, transport them in a large cardboard box, cat basket or dog cage on newspaper on the back seat of the car, not in an airless boot. All the more reason to find a local breeder.

The male of the species

You do not need to keep a cock for your hens to lay eggs, only for fertile ones. Indeed, keeping a cockerel is not recommended to start with as he will just complicate the issue. He will pesters his ladies in the breeding season (he must run with them for at least three weeks in order to guarantee fertile eggs); he may also be frightening, especially to small children; and, of course, your cock will crow.

None of this should put you off if you want to breed from your own organic stock, but wait until you are more experienced. It is unusual to encounter an aggressive rooster, but if you are attacked, pick up the offender immediately in a firm way, and hold him, making sure he understands who is boss. If he repeats his bad behaviour, he may have to go. You can blunt his spurs by taking off the tip of the point with a small hacksaw and smoothing it with a nail file. Overlong claws can also be manicured in this way.

What should you do with excess cockerels? This is the only downside to breeding poultry. You can run two flocks, with two runs and two houses, but remember that the more birds you keep, the bigger the toll they take on your garden. Occasionally you can find a home for a good pure-bred cockerel. All flocks need some new blood every two or three years. Some people take excess cockerels to market, but this is not a good idea. Alternatively, you have to cull them. In the country, you may find a local butcher, breeder or gamekeeper who will do the deed, and you could learn from them how to do this yourself.

Having killed them, do you eat them? Raising domestic animals for the pot is part of country life. Your excess cockerels have had a short but good life and inevitably will make good eating. If you are just hatching chicks for fun, now would be a salient time to remind you not to hatch too many, because there are always more males than females.

Showing your cockerel

Most poultry fanciers are very fond of their cockerels – they are so handsome. You may be tempted to show a particularly fine example at a local poultry show. First, contact the Breed Club of your particular fancy through the Poultry Club of Great Britain (see page 205) and ask for a list of points, checking out the terminology, then visit and chat to other contestants. Breeding, raising and grooming showbirds is another world.

Gardening with hens

No one with a newly established garden should let their hens range free; likewise real plantsmen or gardeners obsessed with bedding plants. However, with proper management it can work. And you will get something back – wonderful organic fertility, very few pests and a happy troupe of birds.

Poultry manure

This contains about twice as much nitrogen as the equivalent weight of cow, pig or horse muck. If added to chicken run debris, i.e. feathers, straw and bedding, and layered amongst other kitchen and garden waste on the heap and left to rot, it is potent stuff. Never put neat manure directly on to plants; let it rest where it will activate your compost. Most of the droppings around the garden will get swept up with leaves or lawn mowings. To disperse messes from a pristine lawn, use a besum broom or blast with a high-powered hose.

Seasonal management

In spring, confine the hens to a run to protect the new growth. Tip all the garden waste in with them to scratch through. Release them in June, and cover vulnerable plants with cloches. When planting catch crops of green manure (alfalfa, comfrey, clover and mustard greens) to improve the soil's structure, let your birds feast and scratch before digging in. Hens find many weeds and seed beneficial and will self-medicate effectively. For instance, they may eat rhubarb leaves as a wormer.

In autumn and winter, they will forage for pests, finish off old veg and windfalls and liberally manure your beds. Fallen leaves can be dried in sacks and used in muddy runs. To prevent pockmarks from dustbathing, provide a site in the run. Hens love to dustbathe in bonfire ashes but check for lit cinders lurking.

Hen health

It is hardly surprising that most poultry problems are caused by stress due to overcrowding and trauma. However, if you give your birds a peaceful life, plenty of space, an organic environment, and adequate food and water, you will be spared most of the textbook disasters.

Looking after sick birds

If a bird is unwell – hunched up, head down, eyes closed – isolate her with access to drinking water in a separate henhouse. Pick her up and hold her. Is she underweight? Feel her crop under her neck; if it is hard, dose her with a little olive oil. Is she straining to lay an egg? A little oil rubbed round the vent will help. If you are unsure, leave her to relax for a while and if she does not perk up, contact your vet. Explain she is a much-loved, organically raised pet.

Preventing health problems

Given an organic environment and stress-free life, your hens should thrive. Treat minor parasites (worms, lice or scaly leg) when the need arises, not as a matter of course. There are organic remedies for these problems, and homeopathy has been found to be particularly effective in dealing with wounds, infections and arthritis. Cider vinegar is also useful as an antiseptic, and mashed garlic in their drinking water protects against worms.

Moulting

All birds moult their feathers annually in early autumn. Your flock will look like broilers first and then porcupines, as the feathers grow back through transparent tubes which then fall away. (Cod-liver or vegetable oil with brown bread is a good tonic.) The henhouse floor will be covered in bushels of feathers. Good layers can go almost naked. Unattractive, their plumage will be back on peak form in time for the breeding season.

Hens do not lay during the moult. Other reasons for not laying include insufficient protein, broodiness, being a mother, bullying, lack of light and stress. Traditionally the egg-laying season is from mid February to early November.

Wing clipping

If you have to confine a hen in the run, she may be flighty and escape; avoid this by clipping a wing. Get someone to hold her while you trim the first four feathers of one wing – they will grow back. Do not wing clip during the moult. To hold a hen correctly, pass your upturned hand under her breast and grasp her legs between your fingers. Use your other hand to steady and stroke her.

If for any reason you have to cull a bird, it is best to call a vet or experienced keeper. With a little luck, all your hens will live long, happy and productive lives providing you with delicious organic eggs, cheerful companionship and enough enthusiasm to try again.

Keeping ducks and geese

Many of the reasons for keeping these lovable waterfowl are the same as those for hens but, apart from their obvious charms, they are also excellent producers of first-rate organic free-range eggs and premium home-raised meat. Ducks and geese are easier to keep than hens, are hardier, less prone to infection, and will live and lay longer. In the wild, they have the best of all worlds: they can walk (or waddle) and fly and swim, but they can be equally happy in a smallholding or a large garden with a pond and as much space as you can spare.

Getting started

Start off by buying a couple of domestic ducks and a drake, or a pair of geese and a gander (geese bully ducks so do not pen them together). Keep them in a run with a pond and as much access to your garden as possible.

In most areas you do not need permission to keep waterfowl, but check first with your local Environmental Health Department. Consult your neighbours to see if they will flock-sit while you are away on holiday and whether they are prepared to put up with the odd quack. Geese can be very noisy and everyone will be aware of any comings or goings.

Preparing for their arrival

If everyone is happy, decide where to site your run and pond. Choose a spot that provides shade and shelter and is as secure from predators as possible. Give up as much space as you can. If not, you are going to have to be especially conscientious and clean out the run and house every day or the occupants' health will suffer. Buy a specially formulated house that is large enough in which to feed them, or adapt an existing garden shed.

Ducks and geese make cheap and easy guests, depending on how much land you offer as grazing, and how much surplus food your household produces. Pure breeds are more expensive than other poultry, especially the ornamentals, so stick to the basic domestic utility strains – unless you are prepared to give them five-star treatment. Go to local shows, charm poultry-keeping friends, scan smallholder magazines and seek out breeders (see page 205). Always visit before buying, order well beforehand and have your run, house and feed ready and waiting before collecting them.

Adopt a routine

Your flock should be fed in the morning inside their shed and left until they lay. Ducks usually lay before 9 am and the eggs are collected daily and eaten fresh. They can then be let out into the run and garden to potter around until sunset when supper is served in their quarters and they are shut up for the night.

Finally, although both ducks and geese are hardy, easy and great fun to keep, you must clean their run regularly and visit them twice a day, although you will be tempted to spend much more time watching them.

Why keep ducks and geese?

- They are suppliers of top-grade fertilizer, soil conditioner and compost activator.
- They are land grazers, lawn mowers and natural burglar alarms.
- They provide chemical-free pest control.
- They are educative and endearing pets for the whole family.

Where to keep your flock

Ducks can see at night and sleep with one eye open and half their brain alert looking out for predators, but, in spite of this, you will still have to protect your domestic waterfowl against predators, such as foxes and dogs, especially if they are big and heavy or cannot fly because you have clipped their wings.

Housing your flock

The ideal waterfowl home is a shed in a netted area with a pond and a gate leading to occasional access to your garden – depending on their security and how fussy a gardener you are. Keep them in a covered run for the first two weeks until they know their address. The smaller breeds (and Muscovies, which fly surprisingly well despite their size) may need the flight feathers on one wing trimmed; ask your breeder to do it. Of course, subsequent generations will not need clipping.

All waterfowl prefer moving water, so a river or stream in your garden is ideal, but you will have to wire net an area right down to the riverbed, to stop your flock sailing away. Visiting wildfowl will be a nuisance and they will inter-breed and steal food.

Protecting against predators

If there are lots of foxes about, then perhaps you should think again. You could try building a run with a wire-netted roof, carefully cutting away any overhanging branches of nearby trees. However, a determined fox will visit every day until eventually you make a mistake and leave the run door open.

Providing a pond

People will try to tell you that it is possible to keep ducks and geese without a pond, but no-one who has seen how ducks take to water would deny them a paddling pool at the very least. They seem content in even the most appalling conditions, but give them the largest pond you can – and don't overcrowd. Remember also that even a shallow pond can be dangerous to small children.

Types of pond

Concrete ponds should be about 30 cm (12 in) deep and cleanable with a hose and broom. You can clean a simple-shaped fibreglass pond by running a hose to overflow. Geese are less aquatic than ducks, so a pair could manage with a large sunken galvanized cistern for preening, but check the level daily or they will develop eye problems.

If you are excavating a pond, use a strong butyl liner, and fold some strong plastic netting, which has been secured with tent pegs round the turf edges, to stop your ducks dabbling the perimeter away. Alternatively, you can protect the banks with flints, logs or flagstones. The water will need topping up during periods of drought.

You can purchase a mail order duck pond. Alternatively you could use a rigid-sided child's paddling pool with a ramp as a temporary paddling pool for older ducklings.

If you live in the countryside, you may find that you have the right to keep a few geese on the village green or pond. Contact your Parish Council to find out.

Providing shade and shelter

Ducks and geese can suffer from sunstroke so they will need access to shady spots. In the average garden, this should not be a problem, but bamboo screens can be erected inside the run. Make sure you provide extra shelter in winter with strategically placed straw bales.

The ideal house

Ducks and geese are very hardy. House them for protection from predators and easy egg collection, rather than five-star comfort. Ducks need 60 sq cm (2 sq ft) per bird in their sleeping quarters; geese need double that space. An ordinary 2.4 m x 1.2 m (8 x 4 ft) garden shed will be fine for housing six ducks or three geese. You should supply a large door as they are wary of small popholes and will not go in to roost or lay.

Unlike hens, waterfowl do not roost above ground at night, so anything above head height is only useful as extra ventilation space. However, it is more important for your own comfort when you muck out and hose down the interior. If you have to crouch down in some discomfort, you will be less inclined to carry out your housekeeping duties.

Keeping the floor dry

Make sure that the floor is kept dry or the occupants will develop problems with arthritis, cramp and rheumatism, especially in their legs and feet. They may also refuse to come in at night. Cover the floor with some sheets of newspaper, then add a good layer of straw or shredded corrugated cardboard (available from your feed merchant) and replace it with fresh every morning. It will rot down nicely on the compost heap. Wash the floor down regularly with a hose, so a concrete flag floor with a drain is the best option.

Create a nesting area

Board in the darkest end of the shed with a 2 m (6 ft) wide floorboard or plank to provide a large nesting area. Keep this space full with a thick, comfortable layer of straw and also a couple of large china broody eggs which will encourage your ladies to lay in the house and not around the run and garden.

Home-made or commercial?

When building your own house for ducks and geese, you should make sure that you protect the wood from damp and rot with organic wood preservative, not creosote which is dangerous to birds. However, if you're not a dab hand at do-it-yourself, there are also several specialist companies that sell purpose-built duck and goose houses. As a general rule, waterfowl housing should be more basic and, hopefully, cheaper than henhouses.

Penning newcomers

If your geese come to you free range and are not used to being housed, then at least pen them at night to keep them safe. You could use a portable wire pen and move it every day to keep the ground fresh. You can encourage reluctant geese to enter the pen at night with a handful of corn.

Choosing a breed

All domestic ducks have been developed from the Mallard, and domestic geese from the wild Grey Lag goose. Pure black or white birds occur naturally; the whites were bred and valued for their paler flesh.

Some breeds were developed for their laying potential: Khaki Campbell ducks can lay almost an egg a day – more than the best hens. Heavy birds, such as the Aylesbury duck and Toulouse goose, were obviously destined for the table. The most decorative birds were bred as ornamentals, and decoy ducks were raised for sport. Muscovies are a separate species.

Start with a pure breed trio – a drake and two ducks or a gander and two geese – and then hatch out some young over the next few years to bring the flock up to numbers that your garden and pond can cope with. A small garden is fine for two ducks or a pair of tiny Call Ducks which come in a variety of colours. Bear in mind that geese mate for life – a span of thirty years – and will be really miserable and will pine if they are separated.

Ducks

When acquiring ducks, it is important to choose a breed that suits your needs: for eggs, for the table, or as garden companions.

Aylesbury (UK)

This duck is pure white with a pinkish-white bill, orange legs and webs (or feet). Perfected over the centuries as a table bird, it weighs up to 4.5 kg (10 lb). It is deep keeled with a low-slung undercarriage in show birds – avoid really big ones. The Aylesbury lays about 100 eggs per year and will breed if not too fat.

Call Duck (Holland)

These are dear little birds – weighing under 800 g (2 lb). They are firm and cobby with a nice round head, but their irritating, constant quack starts at 4 am in summer. They come in various colours, including white, blue, buff, magpie, apricot, silver, mallard and pied. They eat grass and cause little damage in the garden.

Campbell (UK)

Bred originally by a Mrs Campbell in 1900 to lay prodigiously (up to 300 eggs per annum), these are pretty birds. They are slim and active with a sloping carriage. Khaki Campbells, which are light brown, are the most prolific layers and are therefore highly recommended. Campbells also come in white and dark. They are not good sitters or broodies.

Indian Runner (India)

This is the other premier egg layer. The eggs are white and about the same size as a hen's. Very tall and slim, this duck is appealing, timid and curious. It is available in fawn/white, mallard, black, white and chocolate, and plain white.

Pekin (China)

This creamy white duck is almost pale yellow with an orange bill. It is smaller, slimmer and straighter than the Aylesbury. A wide free ranger, it is a good layer but not a sitter. Friendly and inquisitive, it has soft eyes and a smile.

Muscovy (South America)

The drake is much bigger – 5.5 kg (12 lb) – than the 2.75 kg (6 lb) female, and has a knob on his head. He can be aggressive to other drakes. The ducks do not quack and will mate with other breeds, but offspring will be sterile. Muscovies make good parents and broodies with a 32-day incubation period.

Geese

When choosing some geese, you should base your selection on form and function from the following popular breeds.

Embden (Germany)

This large – over 15 kg (30 lb) – white shapely bird is upright and handsome, with an orange beak and legs, the goose of fairy tales and nursery rhymes. It is valued for its meat as well as its down and feathers.

Toulouse (France)

This huge bruiser of the goose world, with low-slung keel and triple chin, is bred for the table and for pâté in France. It should not be allowed to get fat and needs plenty of exercise. It has grey, black and white plumage.

Pilgrim (UK)

This charming English bird was taken to the United States by the Pilgrim Fathers. The gander is pure white and the goose is grey with a black/white back and white bottom. Goslings are easy to sex and simple to keep. With its upright, horizontal stance, it looks as though it is standing on tiptoes.

Chinese (Asia)

This lighter, more shapely goose has a graceful swan-like appearance and a knob on top of its beak like a Muscovy. It lays well but needs protection from the cold. It is available in white with an orange beak, or grey/brown with a black beak. It is especially noisy.

Feeding ducks and geese

In the ideal situation – a paddock, orchard or meadow – with a natural pond or stream, a small flock of ducks or a few geese will thrive with just a little extra regularly supplied food from you. However, ducks will need more attention as they require grain and grit as well as grass.

Food for ducks

Basically, ducks need grain, grit, grass and water. Like hens, they are omnivores and if left to their own devices with the run of a large garden or smallholding, they will balance their own nutritional requirements with just a little help from their owners. They need a diet of organic mixed corn and a little protein, bought as pellets. Do not give them mash, because ducks turn everything to mash. These basic foods are naturally supplemented with insects, worms, slugs and snails (you hope) from the garden, greenstuff from the kitchen and grass from their surroundings.

Offer your ducks grain in a trough in their house for 20 minutes when you get up, and again at sunset; leave them to supplement with natural food. If they live in a run or you are keep them for eggs, feed 80 per cent organic mixed corn to 20 per cent organic duck/goose pellets from your feed merchant.

Galvanized trough feeders and drinkers are more robust than plastic ones, except during really icy weather when several plastic washing up bowls will do the trick. Drinking water is essential for waterfowl; even one day without could be fatal. Grit is naturally available in your garden, but supply it if for any reason your birds are confined to a pen. The maize in mixed corn will bring out the clotted cream colour in Pekin ducks and enhance orange bills, legs and webs.

Ducks also love barley, pasta, boiled rice, wholemeal bread soaked in water, sweet corn and peanuts. Their bills enable them to pick up food delicately or to dabble and sieve by sucking in water. They will eat weeds, windfall fruit, seeds and, unfortunately, garden plants. Keep your grain and pellets in galvanized bins to deter vermin and always make sure that leftover food is put away between feeds.

Food for geese

Geese, as herbivores, are more self-sufficient than ducks and need much larger quantities of grass and a smaller helping of mixed corn. Water and grit are also essential. They work really well in a mixed smallholding because they will graze much shorter grass than other stock. They will also flourish in a large orchard, where they will finish up the fallen fruit.

Geese do not thrive on really long rough grass. If grazing is occasionally unavailable, give them greenery, such as brassicas and salads, and some cooked root vegetables, supplemented with extra corn and pellets.

Eggs

Your own fresh free-range organic duck eggs will be great for cooking – safe and tasty – but you must collect them regularly and be scrupulous with hygiene. Because the shells are more porous than hens' eggs, bacteria can pass through easily, especially if the layers are kept in mucky conditions. So be prepared to clean up daily.

Collecting eggs

Eat them fresh. Most ducks lay before 9 am, so collect the eggs as you let your ladies out, and clean the shells immediately by wiping with a damp cloth. Discard any eggs you find in the run or garden. Don't leave them lying around to attract rats, crows and other vermin. It may also encourage your ducks to go broody and lay away. Change the straw in their nest boxes regularly to prevent eggs getting soiled.

Geese lay any time from mid-winter to mid-summer. Take the eggs from the nest box for cooking if you do not want them for hatching. Take care, however, as geese can be protective of their eggs.

How many eggs?

You can take the first and second clutch of eggs your geese lay for the kitchen, but they will not supply consistently in the way that hens and some breeds of ducks do. You can get 80 eggs a year from Chinese Browns, but not the 300 a year that Khaki Campbells will produce. Of course, goose eggs are bigger, weighing in at a massive 200 g (8 oz) each, as opposed to hens' eggs at 65 g (2½ oz) and ducks' weighing up to 100 g (4 oz).

Ducks lay well for about three years and will then gradually produce less eggs. You do not need a drake for your ducks to lay. Six good laying ducks can supply 30 eggs a week, more than enough for most people's needs.

Colours and cooking

Wild Mallard lay greenish-blue eggs. White ducks produce white eggs and so do Runners. Rouen lay pale green and Campbells lay tinted brown ones. They are ideal for cooking, especially baking, and are good when mixed with hens' eggs for omelettes and scrambled eggs. Eat them fresh, before they are a week old, because they have a short shelf-life. You can eat them boiled, fresh from the nest box, and would be hard pushed to distinguish them from hens' eggs.

Goose eggs can be used in cooking too, and are excellent in quiches, flans and custards, but neither duck nor goose egg whites can be whipped for meringues.

Duck and goose eggs are difficult to sell, but if you have a glut you can contact DEFRA (see page 205) for their advice on sales. It is probably better to use the eggs in baking and put the cakes in the freezer.

Augmenting your flock

Ducks and geese are gregarious birds and introducing newcomers is easy. Just make sure they are kept in a run under cover for two weeks until they get used to their new home. Youngsters without a mum to support them will have to be segregated until they can hold their own, but hatching out your own ducklings or goslings is a natural way to increase your stock.

Ducks

Ducks' eggs are traditionally hatched under broody hens (see page 120), or they can be incubated. Generally, they should be hatched and reared as naturally as possible. A good mum can pass on important information to her brood. Ducks have a bad reputation as mothers, so make sure your broody is at least two years old. Rouens and Muscovies make good mums although, paradoxically, the breeds that lay most make the worst sitters.

Place a couple of broody eggs in the nest box to encourage your duck to lay. Leave her daily eggs until she has a clutch and starts to sit. Remember, not too many or the result will bring chaos to your garden. If you want to try a new breed or do not have a drake, you can buy fertile organic eggs from a breeder. Only set eggs that are less than seven days old and have been kept in a cool place. Ducks' eggs should be turned daily: first to the left, the next day to the right. Reject any damaged, oddly shaped or unusually large or small ones.

The duck will line the nest with soft down plucked from her breast, and cover her eggs when she nips out to feed. If she has laid away and is sitting on a clutch in the garden, she will be vulnerable to predators, hence the term 'sitting duck'. If tame, you may be able to move her, plus nest and a few eggs, to the safety of the run, but she will probably abandon them.

Make sure your broody has enough food and water in the run to immerse her head and that any mess is cleared daily from the nest. The incubation period is 28 days from the time she starts to sit. When the ducklings hatch they will stay under their mother for two days, surviving on food from the egg. After two days, she will lead them out – reward her with a big feed and remove any unhatched eggs. Keep mum and babes in a run with a partially boarded top for shelter, and move it every day to keep the grass fresh. You can open the cage at the end of the first week (closing it again at night), and then let them out into the main run and from there into the garden.

Unlike most birds, parent ducks and geese do not feed their young, except by enthusiastic example. Give your babes ad lib organic duckling or goose crumbs for the first two weeks, and growers pellets thereafter. Clean water should be offered in gradually larger saucers containing a few pebbles, to stop the ducklings jumping in and chilling.

Geese

Goose eggs have a low hatching rate. The mother goose will behave in the same way as a duck, reluctant to leave a nest with eggs. Encourage her to do so just once a day to feed and drink. The eggs have a 30–32 day incubation period and take some time to chip out. Don't be tempted to help the goslings hatch. The gander will wander around outside like an expectant father. He can be reunited with his family after two days. Both parents are fiercely protective, so be careful. Feed the goslings little and often with organic goose crumbs, boiled rice and chopped lettuce. Geese can be left to bring up their young without help.

Geese are xenophobic and unwelcoming to newcomers, so the only way to augment your flock is to hatch. You should use introduced fertile eggs to bring in new bloodlines.

Drakes and ganders

Unlike cocks, drakes get on quite well together although they bicker in the mating season. You should not have too many or your ducks will get pestered. In some breeds, the duck and drake are similar – the male is a little bigger with a couple of curled tail feathers. In others (with Mallard in their make-up), the sexes look completely different: the males are handsome whereas the females are dowdy so as not to attract attention when sitting.

Drakes should be kept with their wives for at least four weeks to ensure the eggs are fertile. Increase the percentage of layers pellets for the females; the drakes will need little encouragement to mate. They are legendarily promiscuous and indulge in comical display behaviour. Some breeds prefer water for successful lovemaking but most will mate anywhere, especially in groups.

Drakes start to pair up in January, and the ducks will go broody as the weather warms up. One drake can cope with four to eight ducks, although often it is the other way round. In the wild, ducks are monogamous, but domestication has made them bigger, tamer and oversexed. All ducks will crossbreed, and often your pure breed will fall for some free-flying Romeo wild Mallard.

Ganders can live for 30 years, are faithful to their mates and not ready to breed until they are two or three years of age. They are usually bigger than their wives and often have different plumage. They can be aggressive, standing protectively between you and their flock, stretching out their necks and hissing. During the mating season, geese are very bellicose and, while offspring are hatched and reared, you may need to carry a stick. Don't let young children go near ganders at this time.

Excess drakes and ganders are usually culled for their meat, especially for Christmas feasts. Duck-meat is best killed young, while goose-meat has more flavour in a two-year-old bird. Ducks should always have their necks pulled whereas geese should be stunned before slitting their throats; both will need expert attention. This is hard to contemplate as ducks and geese are very appealing. However, at least you will know they have had a good life, and the meat will be free range, organic and probably very tasty.

Garden companions

Ducks and geese would not be most people's first choice as co-gardeners, but if you are going to keep them, it is important that you allow them as much space as you possibly can. Ideally, access to a paddock, orchard, wood or an area of wild garden would be the best habitat.

If your entire garden is under cultivation, you could give your ducks limited access for a couple of hours a day, or maybe during the autumn or winter months. You can only tolerate geese as co-smallholders: they need more grazing than most people's lawns can offer, and it is not possible to share your garden with them if it is too small.

Protecting your garden

The two main problems are the trample factor – ducks and geese have big feet – and the mess, especially round ponds. Lawns can be cleaned with a besom broom or a quick burst of a high-speed hose, but dealing with goose mess can become your worst nightmare. Protect vulnerable areas with wire cages and cloches. Seious gardeners, be warned! Ducks may well eat the compost in your raised beds, and virtually anything that is green and sappy will be nibbled or trampled to the ground.

Say goodbye to frogs, frogspawn and any other pond wildlife. You can keep an extra pond, covered with weld-mesh wire panels, so the wildlife can creep through and plants poke out. Ducks and lily ponds are incompatible. Plant hardy, vigorous water greenery with their roots protected with sacking.

The benefits

On the upside, ducks eat many garden pests, especially slugs and snails and their eggs. Their droppings fertilize the soil and their bedding and feathers make excellent organic compost and soil conditioner when added to the heap in layers with other garden waste. However, although they can do more good than harm in gardens, keep them out of the vegetable plot. Geese will keep grass down in rough areas and eat a variety of grassland weeds, although not tough grasses, docks, thistles or nettles.

Ducks mix well with hens, ignoring them unless they have babies, but don't pen or house them together. Ducks are bullied by geese, so give them plenty of escape routes. Train your cats and dogs to tolerate them and co-exist happily, but other people's pets can be a problem. Foxes are the worst predators and you may have bad experiences with herons. Ducklings are tempting to hawks, mink, squirrels, rats and stoats. Apart from uncontrolled dogs and foxes, most animals give geese a wide berth.

Keeping wildfowl encourages other birds to visit your land. Duck and goose feathers will line their nests, and swallows will gather mud from the banks of your pond. Ducks will work your lawn, darting to catch flies and midges.

Staying healthy

Ducks and geese seem to be amazingly hardy creatures, and they can thrive with very little input from their owners. Give them as much space as you can or the land will get infested with worms. If your birds are not thriving and you suspect worms, your vet can supply a remedy. Garlic in their drinking water is a good preventative.

Preventing problems

Provide lots of clean water for drinking and preening or your birds will get sore eyes. If kept on the hard with little opportunity to swim, they can get corns and calluses on their feet, and both geese and ducks may develop arthritis if their bedding is left to rot and gets damp. Homeopathy provides several good remedies, including bryonia, and a massage with warm olive oil can help. Isolate any lame bird in a separate coop, with plenty of bedding and lots to eat and drink, until she recovers. All birds can catch lung diseases from damp bedding, so make sure yours sleep on dry straw, not hay, which can harbour fungal bacteria. Both arnica and calendula cream are useful treatments for healing wounds.

In summer, your flock must have access to shady spots, as sunstroke is not uncommon, especially if their water supply dries up as well. Isolate in the shade with plenty of water if you notice a bird sitting with laboured breathing.

Catching and handling

Like hens, ducks and geese are very difficult to catch. They always know what you have in mind. Trap them by building a wire cage and feeding them ever nearer and then inside it before dropping the door, but this takes about a week. You can catch them in their house at night, but if you need them immediately, use an angler's fish landing net. Geese are very unbiddable, and the best way is to herd them into a cage with long sticks.

Move slowly among your birds, and talk to them. Ducks are inquisitive, friendly creatures but suspicious of things that move. Geese vary and should always be approached with care.

To handle a bird, slide one hand under the tummy and hold the legs, keeping the neck gently under your arm. Watch out for sharp claws, especially on Muscovies. Use your other arm to steady and stroke her. If you need to transport ducks or geese, put them in a strong ventilated cardboard box or dog cage, lined with lots of newspaper, and place on the back seat of the car, rather than in an airless boot.

Moulting

Ducks and geese moult from September through to November and your garden will be full of feathers. Never clip wings or trim feathers during the moult.

Keeping livestock

Livestock can provide us with valuable companionship, manure, food and clothing, but they also require your daily attention. If you want a smallholding to be properly alive, then you need to keep stock; but if work or holidays take you away from home, you should think long and hard before starting. Illnesses, escapes and births are no respecters of your busy schedule, and they generally will occur at the most awkward moments. However, if you have resolved to go ahead, you must decide which animals will best suit your circumstances. For instance, pigs can be kept in the least space; a few sheep, well fenced in, are best if you want some grassland kept tidy; goats are great at turning small areas of rough grazing into adequate supplies of milk for a small family; and, if you have enough acreage, having your own cow is very special.

Pigs

Many of us do not like the idea of eating our own animals. However, it is said that every bit of the pig can be eaten except the squeal, and also that you should keep your pig with love and eat him with love. Pigs are delightful to keep and really will eat and grow on just about anything.

Organic pigs eat all sorts of supposed wastes, enjoy their relative freedom and varied diet (and the time you spend talking to them and scratching them) and produce valuable manure and delicious pork, bacon, sausages, brawn, and more. The best way to start is to get a few weaners between eight and ten weeks old which are ready to leave their mothers. Look in the local paper or check the Soil Association database (see page 206).

Breeds

If you aspire to pedigree breeding, then breed is obviously of prime importance, but if not, it matters little. The more old-fashioned the breed, the more resilient the pig but the fatter the meat. Gloucester Old Spots, Wessex Saddlebacks, Berkshires and Tamworths are all distinctive and hardy; Welsh, Middle and Large Whites, and Durocs are still suitable although a bit more modern; but the Landrace is a bit too streamlined for the organic smallholder.

Make sure that however many pigs you buy, half of them or at least one is female. Then, when they are big enough to kill and eat, you can decide whether to get ambitious and keep one or more to breed your own weaners. If you have room, there is a lot to be said for keeping a sow; she will produce about 18 piglets a year (in two lots of nine), so you can keep a couple to eat and sell the rest at weaning for some useful cash, or even keep them and sell the meat to your neighbours.

Housing

For growing pigs, housing is very simple and can be made of any old materials, such as scrap timber and corrugated iron sheets, but it must be strong. The young need a snug, weatherproof lying area, well littered up with straw, where they can make a nest and lie in a heap, as well as an outside run. At the minimum, this will be a patch of concrete where you can feed them and where they will choose a dunging area which you will clean up regularly.

Hopefully, you will be able to let them run out and dig up and manure a patch of ground. Fence it in with two strands of electric wire, 10 and 20 cm (4 and 8 in) from the ground. Alternatively, put up some pig netting, using stout posts. Either way, make sure you keep them off the lawn.

Breeding sows must have their own space, with room to lie down and turn around, and each hut must be weatherproof. You'll need access from each end, just in case you have to help at farrowing, as she may lie either way, so there is an opening for her at one end and a trap door where you can reach in at the other. Buy half-round arcs ready made, or make them yourself from half-round galvanized sheets. You can make triangular section ones, using a timber frame and Sterlingboard for the roof and sides.

Feeding

Pigs are omnivorous, but don't feed them any meat or animal by-products. They will eat and enjoy grass, weeds and all your vegetable waste. Potatoes and their peelings should be boiled.

If you cannot let them run out and dig up the ground, you must give your pigs some soil to eat to prevent iron deficiency. Do this by chucking some turf into their pen.

In addition, especially for young growing pigs and nursing mothers, you will need to feed more concentrated sources of energy and protein, such as ground cereals – mainly wheat or barley as pigs are not very keen on oats. If you have your own cow or goat, you may well have some surplus or waste whole or skimmed milk. This makes an ideal protein supplement – pigs love it poured on their cereal. (Whey is very popular, too, but it is mainly lactose with very little protein.) Dried skimmed milk is also excellent. If not, ground beans or soya meal will be good at a ratio of around 3:1 cereal to pulse.

Most feeds can be obtained in organic form from your local feed mill, or buy a premixed pig ration, usually in the form of 'nuts', known as 'sow and weaner' or 'pig rearer'.

How much food?

When the pigs are foraging and/or having various scraps, it is hard to be precise about rations and amounts — use your judgement. Heavily lactating sows and pigs under 45 kg (100 lb) can eat more or less ad lib but dry sows and older growing pigs need to be restricted or they will get too fat. So, feed your little pigs a little twice a day and increase it as they clear it up, until they reach 45 kg (100 lb). Give them enough to keep them in good condition and growing steadily. They will always demand more but try not to overdo it.

Feed lactating sows generously – about 2.7 kg (6 lb) per day if foraging or up to 5.5 kg (12 lb) if not, or even 9 kg (20 lb) if they have a big litter and no other food. Cut right back to 1–2 kg (2–4 lb) when you take the piglets off. Then see that they maintain their condition without getting fat as their pregnancy develops.

Creep feeding

When the piglets are two or three weeks old, they will get interested in their mother's food. At this stage, start 'creep feeding'. If they are electric fenced, fence off an area within the overall run with one high strand. The piglets will go under this but the sow will not. Here you can have a trough just for them, so they can feed without competing with mum. Or make a fence with a small hole in it.

All stock need access to clean water. Pigs chew and knock over plastic troughs, so use an old sturdy sink or cast iron trough. You can buy pig drinkers which you plumb in, but don't leave plastic hose exposed to the pigs' teeth.

Illness

It is unlikely that your organic free-range pigs will suffer from disease. They may get digestive upsets if they overfeed on something, but a little fasting should put that right. Injuries can also happen: piglets can get squashed by their mothers, hurt fighting, or stuck in a trough. Use the appropriate homeopathic remedy as for humans for threating these. Slit an apple, put the remedy inside, and feed the apple to the pig. You can also give a constitutional remedy if you think that it is appropriate: most pigs will respond to Antimonium Crudum.

Breeding

A sow should go to the boar for the first time when she is approaching a year old. She will come on heat for a day or so every 18–24 days. You need to find someone who will lend you their boar, take in your sow(s) for service, or perhaps share a boar with you.

Farrowing

Conception should happen the first time the boar and sow mate. Gestation is three months, three weeks and three days from conception. Sometimes a sow can be confused about her first farrowing and may lose some piglets but should cope at subsequent farrowings. Put straw in her hut and she will make a nest with it, lie on her side and pop out the piglets.

Disturb her as little as possible, but you can creep up to the hut to check that all is well and no piglets have got lost or stuck. If you interfere, be quiet, careful and quick. You don't want to upset or distract her.

However, if she is not making any progress, or has had a few and then none, you may need to slip a hand in and check that there is not a piglet stuck sideways. If there is, turn it and pull it out; the next few will probably come out in a rush. If you are lucky they will all be alive, but one or two may be dead. Alternatively, call the vet.

Rearing piglets

Most piglets grow and develop happily. You will hear the sow tell them when she is going to get up and lie down, and in a well-ordered family there should be few squashings. If you hear frantic squealing, go and check.

Sometimes you get very large litters of up to 18 piglets. If two sows farrow at the same time, you can swap piglets over from one to the other to even up numbers without upsetting either sow if you do it soon after birth. You can also bottle-rear piglets on goat's milk; cow's milk is not so good. For the first few days, put a board across the hut entrance which the sow can climb over but the piglets cannot, or they may wander out and get lost.

Wean the piglets at eight weeks when they are beginning to chew the sow's teats. When they go into the creep area to feed, back a livestock trailer in and put the feed trough in the trailer. They will soon get used to going in to feed. Then, at feeding time, feed the sow in her area, feed the piglets in the trailer, shut the tailgate and drive off. She will hardly notice. Reintroduce the sow to the boar as soon as possible after weaning, and the cycle can start over again.

Sheep

Sheep are possibly the hardest of the farm animals to look after, but they are well worth the effort. Not only do they graze your land and make efficient lawnmowers but they also provide us with succulent meat and valuable wool. If you are seriously considering keeping sheep it would be a good idea to attend a suitable course at your local agriculture college.

The 'golden hoof'

Sheep need no housing; they positively dislike the indoors and will keep grassland tidily mown while manuring fields evenly. They are brilliant at tidying up a grass reseed – once it has come up, let them feed it off; when it recovers, let them feed it off again. Eventually it will be a proper sward and not the weedy mess it was at first. Wherever sheep have grazed, the grass comes up greener, and where they have fed off greens or roots the following crop is better.

Breeds

There are dozens of breeds, and your choice is huge. Try to go for a local breed, which is best adapted to your environment, and through which you will meet other enthusiasts.

If you plan to milk your sheep, rather than just keep them for meat and wool, there is a restricted choice, revolving mainly around crosses of Finns and Dorset Horns. If wool is your main criterion, then your choice will be determined by the type of wool you want, such as a Jacob, which is brown and white, or a brown, tweedy Hebridean. If you live in a temperate, lowland area and want to lamb in autumn or early winter, keep Dorset Horns (or

Poll Dorsets, which are Dorset without horns). If you want no wool at all, have Wiltshire Horns; and if you want a compact, sensible, prolific sheep with a white face and fleece and good conformation, try the new Lleyn breed.

As a rule, mountain breeds are wilder, hardier and slower-growing than lowland ones. If you like succulent young lamb, opt for the Down breeds; if your taste is for mutton and you are prepared to wait, you will like the mountain ones. There are in-between types, like the Clun, which produce particularly good and tasty meat from hoggets (year-old lambs).

Housing

You need only a shelter for use at lambing time, and somewhere to put a sick animal in need of special attention. The lambing shelter should have some pens to protect young families from the wind, rain and snow while the lambs are finding their feet. Make them out of straw bales and old tarpaulins.

Fencing

Sheep really do like to stray and soon get lost with no particular desire to return home so secure fencing is essential. Most sheep will make holes in most hedges, so wire is usually needed, too. Multistrand electric (three strands for ewes and lambs; two for ewes alone) can be effective as long as there is a good 'kick' at all times. You can buy simple fence testers which shine up a coloured light for every 1,000 volts. Sheep need 5,000 to get the message through their fleeces. You must earth the fencer well, keeping the wires free of any vegetation which may short it out.

Alternatively, put up sheep netting, with one or two strands of barbed wire above if you have cattle in the field. Keep it strained tight, using strutted straining posts every 50 m (160 ft) or change of direction, and ordinary stakes every 3 m (9 ft). A good fence will last for years without much maintenance but you may consider fencing like this around your boundaries and using electricity internally.

Feeding

Sheep are very efficient grazers and they will often thrive on fields that look quite bare. Nutritional requirements vary between breeds. As with all stock, you can work out the theoretical requirement but is not so easy to know whether you are achieving it, so you need to observe the condition of your flock and their behaviour. Unlike other stock, sheep may not tell you when they are short but just go on grazing while steadily losing condition.

Tupping and lambing

When sheep are dry and empty, they must be prepared for tupping (service or mating). This process (flushing) involves putting them onto good pasture or introducing supplementary feed, such as turnips or other roots, a cereal such as oats, or purchased nuts, for a couple of weeks before, and during, tupping.

After tupping, grazing, supplemented by good hay if the pastures are bare or snow-covered, will be fine until about two months before lambing. Put the hay in a rack and move it every day to prevent muddy patches. Thereafter you need to supplement your sheep's diet. Unless there is plenty of grass, you should top up the hay rack and give the sheep a 16 per cent protein mix or some nuts. The exception to this is very late lambing, as happens in May, when the spring grass may be adequate on its own.

Lactating ewes

After lambing, the ewes need to be well fed and the ideal is clovery ley or pasture. They will have big appetites and the lambs will soon start to graze as well. In early spring, you may need to carry on with the supplementary feeding until the grass is growing well, but from April onwards your grazing, which should not have had any sheep on it for the winter at least, should be adequate on its own. This is good because ewe feeding time can be confusing for young lambs.

Weaning

When the time comes for weaning, midway between lambing and tupping, the ewes should go onto something bare, while the lambs stay on the good grazing or move to fresh. Hopefully, you will have enough grazing to get the lambs to the right weight and condition for slaughter; if not, you can grow some roots for them or introduce some concentrate. If you enjoy mutton, you have to keep them ticking over through the winter and finish them on brassica tops or spring grazing. If you only have a few sheep and one field, the general principles still apply.

Breeding

Most lambing takes place in the spring. The gestation period is five months minus about a week. October tupping (mountain breeds) gives March lambing; Down ewes will take the ram in late July and lamb after Christmas; and Dorset Horns/Poll Dorsets can lamb almost any time and are often lambed in October or November. In all other breeds, fertility tails off after early December so there is not much lambing after the middle of May.

If you lamb in March and April, then your grazing requirement will peak when the grass is growing fastest, you will be drying off your ewes in July/August when the grass tends to dry up, and you should be able to finish the last of your lambs and flush your ewes on autumn grass.

If you only have a few ewes you will not want to keep an underemployed and rapidly depreciating ram all the year, so you can borrow someone's ram when he is not busy at home or send your ewes to your neighbour when he is. Whenever it happens, the ewes should come on heat every 16 days and should be with the ram for at least two heats.

Preparing for lambing

As lambing approaches, make a temporary shelter or clean out and disinfect a space in a permanent building with clean straw available. Only use traditional wattle hurdles for one lambing as they can carry infection. You may not need to use these pens (most ewes never come in) but they can be invaluable. Driving rain can finish off baby lambs before they have found their feet. If a young lamb gets chilled and is unable to suckle, take it indoors and warm it up with a fan heater or hair dryer. If wet, rub it well with a towel.

Lambing

You may also need to catch a ewe and lamb her if, after about an hour's lambing, she is not progressing. You will need some lambing gloves and gel and a manual to help you in case of malpresentations.

Homeopathic remedies can be very useful: Caulophyllum for ringwomb or if the ewe has not opened up enough; arnica and aconite for bruising and shock after a hard lambing; pulsatilla for a white discharge after lambing; or pyrogen for a septic one.

Expect to lose one or two lambs and don't be disheartened when the inevitable happens. If you get triplets, rejoice but watch them very carefully. If another ewe has a single or loses one it is worth trying an adoption.

As soon as you are sure that there is not another lamb, take away the ewe's own lamb and smear the adoptee with the ewe's birth juices and plug him on. When he has sucked, introduce the real lamb, who must not be left

too long before getting his feed of colostrum – it may or may not work. If it seems to be working, keep the family away from the rest of the flock until they are totally bonded.

Buying in lambs

If all goes well, you can go out a week or two later and watch the lambs charging happily round the field while the ewes contentedly graze. However, if you decide that this is all too complicated, there are alternatives. The simplest is to buy 'store lambs' from a friendly organic farmer. These are half or more grown and you can just grow them on till they are ready to eat; or you could pick up some orphan lambs from a busy shepherd and bottle rear them. They can have a little shelter in the corner of a field, and eventually grow up on grazing.

Disease

Sheep in general, and growing lambs in particular, are at risk from internal and external parasites, and clostridial and other infections, from which they have to be protected and treated if the protection fails.

Worms

There are various worms which can damage, sometimes fatally, sheep's insides. They have different life cycles but all alternate between the grazing animals and the pasture, so that one sheep passing worms or eggs in its dung infects another which picks them up while grazing. The first control strategy is 'clean grazing', i.e. the grazing used for ewes and

lambs in the spring must have been free from sheep for at least a year. At weaning, some fresh clean land, which has had no sheep for as long as possible and certainly not earlier in the same season, must be found for lambs. It is an advantage to have other stock, to shut up land for haymaking, and have grass leys in rotation with vegetable or cereal crops. If this is impossible, mixed grazing, where the sheep graze with cattle, can help by diluting the stocking rate of the sheep and spreading them more thinly on the ground.

If the ewes are carrying worms, the clean grazing system will break down as they will infect the pastures and thence the lambs. Any sheep you bring in must be clean and should be wormed in advance. Do not use ivermectin types which kill dung beetles; your vet will advise on 'white wormers'. Keep a close eye on the lambs as they grow and at any signs of scouring (loose dung), take dung samples and get the vet to do a worm count and advise if a wormer is needed. Ideally, you don't want to use wormers but must keep your lambs healthy.

A further problem that causes sickness and death in lambs is coccidiosis, which they can pick up from their pasture. For this reason, you should, as well as having clean grazing to move on to, not use the same patch of ground for lambing in consecutive years.

Clostridials

These soil-living diseases can cause severe or fatal illness. Often the first sign is a dead lamb, followed by another and another. You may either not have them in your land or have them at a very low level. If you do not have problems, there is no need to vaccinate. If, however, you find any sickly or dead lambs, take them to the vet straightaway and get a diagnosis or post-mortem. If necessary, you can usually vaccinate all the other lambs and give them rapid protection. You then have to decide on a future policy with your vet, which may involve vaccinating the pregnant ewes every year and/or the young lambs. This, like regular worming, feels rather unorganic, but may be unavoidable. If possible, start your enterprise on land that has not carried sheep for many years.

External parasites

Blow flies are large and green and lay their eggs in the fleece, at any time from May to October. The eggs develop into maggots which bore into the flesh. If you see a sheep twisting its head back towards its tail, catch it and look for a dark patch in the fleece. Cut the wool away and there will be the maggots. Remove the wool around the affected area and clean off all the maggots. Treat the wounded area with something antiseptic and fly-repellent, such as tea tree ointment or powder. Infection can develop rapidly and the sheep becomes ill and septic. Give her Pyrogen 30 three times a day until she recovers. If you catch the problem early, you can let her back into the flock; keep an eye for a few days.

If your ewes are clean and healthy, they are unlikely to be troubled much by blowfly unless shearing is delayed. Lambs are very vulnerable if they get 'shitty-arsed', so keep the worms

down. Summer the sheep in an open, dry, airy field as flies favour sheltered, warm, damp areas. If these precautions fail, treat 'at-risk' animals with an approved pyrethroid.

It is important to make sure that the sheep you buy are scab free, and also that you maintain good fences so that they are unable to mix with others. If one of your sheep is itching and losing its fleece, you should consult your vet immediately.

Footrot and scald

There are preventative actions that you can take that will reduce or eliminate these health problems. You should trim your sheep's feet twice a year or more frequently if the ground is wet and/or their feet are soft, and you see any lameness. Keep them out of mud. If they are drinking, put footrot nosode in the water, and also use a formalin footbath at three per cent concentration.

Shearing

Shearing takes place between May and July, depending on breed and altitude, and is normally done by itinerant (often Antipodean) shearers, although it is perfectly possible to do your own using hand shears. If you sell the fleeces to the Wool Board they will hardly cover the cost of shearing, but if you can spin and weave they can be much more valuable and end up as the most environmentally-friendly clothing you can wear. So why not have a go and try your hand out at making your own clothes?

Cows

The advantage of having a cow is you get raw, organic milk; the downside is the commitment to milking twice a day. Keeping a suckler cow is not very demanding but rearing calves requires more work in the first few weeks.

Breeds

These are divided into dairy, dual purpose and beef. The most popular dairy breed is the Holstein Friesian, which is big, kindly, black and white, and produces large quantities of milk. A typical Friesian gives eight gallons a day at peak and averages over four gallons a day through lactation. She will need two acres for grazing and hay, as well as a ton of rolled cereals and proteins. Unless you have a huge family, she is not the ideal house cow.

Moving down in size and redder in colour are Ayrshires and Dairy Shorthorns, still capable of substantial yields of richer milk, then the Channel Island breeds: Guernseys and Jerseys. These produce milk with very high butter fat. Guernseys are large and very quiet; Jerseys are petite but surprisingly tough. You can keep two of them instead of one Holstein Friesian.

Dairy Shorthorns are so called to distinguish them from Beef Shorthorns, but they are beefier than other dairy breeds – quiet and robust. The Gloucester is a rare, relatively undeveloped dairy breed, which does not produce a lot of milk nor need masses of food. The only British breeds regarded as dual purpose are the South Devon and Red Poll. South Devons are big and produce Channel Island-type milk; Red Polls have reasonable yields and good beef calves.

Crossbred cattle

There are many of these as dairy farmers usually use beef sires, such as Hereford and Angus, on their poorer cows. Consider them if buying stores or calves. Do not buy Limousin crosses: the pure-breds are nice but the crosses are wild. A good place to assess different breeds is your local agricultural show, where you can meet the breeders as well as the stock. There are organic herds of most breeds.

Housing

If you have good hedges, then you can keep suckler cows and calves or stores with no housing at all, although you will need a stall or crush where you can restrain an animal for special treatment, such as foot-trimming, or a visit from your veterinary surgeon.

A dairy cow prefers to have a cow shed but will be fine outside. If you house her, even just at night, she could use at least a ton of straw for bedding in a winter. If you are not on light land and you leave her out, she may make a mess of your grassland, reducing its productivity in spring. You will have to bring her in to milk her, and you'll need somewhere for her calf, unless you let it run with her all the time.

A loosebox similar to a horse's stable is ideal; a concrete floor is not essential if you use plenty of straw. Keep her, and any calves, dry and out of draughts but with plenty of ventilation, and let them out in the daytime whenever ground conditions allow.

A good system if you keep the calf is to milk the cow in the evening, let her stay in with the calf and her hay at night, then milk her in the morning and let her out to graze. Cows defecate as soon as they get up so if you keep them in at night, be generous with straw bedding and muck out regularly. Stack the strawy dung outside, turn it once or twice at monthly intervals to get it to compost into good manure for your fields or garden. Keep hay and straw dry under a tarpaulin or in a shed.

Fencing

Dairy cattle can be trained to respect electric fences and kept in with one strand carrying 3,000 volts. They can eat the grass under the wire, so trim any weeds which may grow up and short the fence. Beef animals with woolly coats may not be so obliging and may need three strands of barbed wire to restrain them.

Feeding

Producing milk takes a lot of energy and protein, so modern cattle are bred to eat well. Cows like to go out, fill up and then lie down and have a good long cudding session. So they need plenty of grazing and, whenever it is short, a good supply of hay or silage.

Silage making and feeding is not feasible on a small scale; you will have to buy or make hay. The better the hay, the more cattle eat and thrive. When planning a feeding regime, note that half your grass will grow between mid-April and mid-June, so you will have a surplus then or a shortage for the rest of the year.

Haymaking

If you have two acres available for your cow and calf, use an electric fence to keep her on half an acre in the spring while you make hay on the rest; allow her more as she needs it. You may struggle to make this amount of hay by hand, so try to find a local farmer to do it for you, preferably with a baler.

Making your own hay is worth considering if you have surplus grass; good organic hay in small bales commands a high price. The art is to catch the right weather. Cut at the beginning of a fine spell any time after the beginning of June, turn the grass daily until it feels crackly, bale it, and get it in before it rains. This sounds easy, but if it is a bit wet the grass may go mouldy; if it is still green it may heat so much it catches fire! If rain is imminent and the hay is not 'fit', roll it up as if for baling and then spread it out again when the sun comes out.

If rain is due and the hay is not quite fit for a small baler, roll it up with a round net-wrap baler and leave the bales out to cure for a few weeks. Or use other stock like store cattle or sheep to eat the spring grass, and buy in the hay. You should have 150 small bales per cow.

Supplements

Grazing and hay are adequate for beef cattle and growing heifers, but calves and milkers need supplementation. You can't feed modern cows a poor diet and ask them to produce a small amount of milk – that's not what they are bred for; they will just produce more milk than they should and lose condition, with consequent loss of health and fertility. Better to feed a cow generously without force-feeding and keep her in reasonable condition – relating what you feed her to how much milk she produces. Very roughly, almost unlimited fresh spring grass with a little hay will give a cow maintenance and enough energy and protein for up to 23 litres (40 pints) milk a day, while unlimited hay with a little autumn grazing may be worth 4.5 or 9 litres (8 or 16 pints). The shortfall will come from purchased concentrate, either from a local organic farmer or a merchant. Higher protein levels encourage milk production while lower levels lead to less milk but help maintain condition. Feed it little and often and never more than 7 kg (16 lb) per day; a dual-purpose cow will give less milk and need less concentrate than a dairy type.

Try growing some kale or fodder beet for winter feed: both are excellent. Do not let your cow get too fat in late lactation. When she is dry, give her poor or restricted grazing and some hay, or even good straw, until three weeks before calving when you should be more generous with the hay and start concentrate feeding at 1–1.5 kg (2–3 lb) per day until she calves, after which you can gradually increase the concentrate level.

Feeding calves

Calves should be suckled for at least 12 weeks (no more than a gallon a day). Start giving hay as soon as they can eat it. They normally start eating concentrate at three weeks, building up to around 1.5 kg (3 lb) per head at weaning. How long you keep them on a cow after 12 weeks is up to you. They can do fine without any milk but can benefit from a little milk for up to six months longer if you can spare it. If on a cow, they will do fine outside; if not, it is better to keep them in until they are six months. When you turn them out in the spring, reduce their feed gradually down to nothing over a few days as they get used to grazing. All stock benefit from plenty of minerals. These can be supplied by herbs, weeds and clover in the pasture, and in winter by seaweed meal.

Disease

Cattle are much easier to keep healthy than sheep, but there are still plenty of things that can go wrong. Prevention is better than cure.

Worms

In their first year, cattle are subject to stomach and lung worms but they can build up lifelong resistance. Calves being turned out on their own need grass that has had no cattle all the previous grazing season. Later in the season they can go onto pasture with a low level of infection, i.e. grazed by adult cattle, to develop resistance. If you run calves with cows, the worm burden is diluted and they develop resistance. If any calves show signs of scouring or coughing, ask your vet for a wormer. Give two monthly doses of husk nosode to protect against lungworm. Liver fluke can be a problem on wet ground so keep areas round water troughs dry. Do not graze boggy areas in September.

Pneumonia

This mainly affects young housed cattle. Symptoms are coughing, raised temperature, rapid breathing and mucous discharges. To prevent it, keep buildings dry, well ventilated and well littered up, and give cows an outside run if possible. Homeopathy is effective, but you must study the cow's behaviour to get the right remedy. If she jumps up when you go in it is probably Phosphorous; if she lies down it will be Bryonia. If in doubt, ask your vet.

Scours

Various organisms cause scouring, but most of the nasty ones, like BVD and Salmonella, are found in more intensive situations. If your calves have had plenty of colostrum at the outset and have suckled since, they should have good immune systems. Scouring can be caused by too much milk, so restrict their milk intake and avoid dehydration by giving electrolyte powder in warm water. Remedies like China can help. If a calf does not recover in a few days, call the vet. To reduce the build-up of infections, clean out looseboxes at least every month; disinfect them before littering up again.

Externals

Flies can be a nuisance and can carry New Forest Eye, which can lead to blindness. It should be treated with Euphrasia and Silica. Ticks are a problem of rough grazing and can carry disease; the worst is Redwater. If you are in a Redwater area, buy stock from affected farms which carry the immunity. There are various forms of tick fever, which usually produce a high temperature for a few days without lasting damage. Stock will be immune thereafter and should pass on the immunity to their offspring.

Breeding

You could buy a cow in milk, but you will probably start with an in-calver and get her settled in before she calves. The best place to calve is out in the field and she will probably do it without any trouble. She will start by pushing out her 'water bag'. As a general rule, give her three hours after that to calve before getting worried. Try not to disturb her but observe what is showing – hopefully, two feet followed by a nose. If there is no nose, and the feet are upside down, the calf is coming backwards and should by pulled away or it will choke as it starts to breathe. If it is more complicated than this, maybe a head back, tail first or twins, get experienced help.

Three life-threatening events can occur after a calving: prolapse, when the womb comes out; haemorrhage, where a vein bursts and blood pours out; and milk fever, when the cow suffers a calcium deficiency and cannot stand up. Call the vet immediately and, in the case of the first two, while you are waiting, give her repeated doses of Aconite to relieve the shock. If there is a haemorrhage, reach in to find where the blood is coming from and stem the flow with your fingers. The vet will put the prolapse back in, or repair the broken vein, or give the cow Calcium Boroglucinate.

Once the cow has licked off the calf, it will soon get up and find a teat. Make sure it does so and gets a good feed of colostrum within six hours of birth. Leave the cow and calf together for 48 hours before your first milking.

Milking

You can buy little one-cow milking machines, but by the time you set it up at the start and wash it up at the end, you might as well milk her by hand. Your choice of cow is important. Modern dairy cows are bred for machine milking and have smaller teats than their ancestors. You want a cow with big teats that you can get your hands around; you are more likely to find one in a Shorthorn or Red Poll herd than a Holstein or a Jersey. When you choose a cow, pick a placid one with big teats.

Bring your cow in for milking and secure her. Give her some food if you like. Approach her from her off-side, bend down and, with your left hand on her flank, try each teat in turn by squeezing the top between the first finger and thumb and sliding them down. Do this a few times and let the milk squirt on to the floor or into a strip cup, just to see that there are no clots or blood in it. Wash each teat with clean water and dry with a paper towel. This will prepare the cow and induce her to give her milk down.

Sit on a stool with a bucket between your knees and your head tucked into the cow's flank. Grab a teat in each hand and squeeze alternately. Depending on the length of the teat, you will use some or all of your fingers against your thumb and palm; if you use too many you will close off the bottom of the teat and the milk cannot get out. You'll know when

you have got it and you hear a continuous purr while the froth mounts up in the bucket. Milk one side, then the other; work round to empty each quarter; many cows have more milk in the back than the front. Then strip out each quarter so that the udder is really slack.

Mastitis

Between you and the calf you must keep the udder emptied regularly. This way your cow will go on making fresh milk for you, and the risk of mastitis is minimized. Don't worry if you see blood in the milk of a fresh-calver; this is quite natural and will clear up in a few days. Blood clots are more worrying, as are any other coloured clots and/or hardness, heat or swelling in one quarter, as these are indicators of mastitis. If this occurs, strip out the quarter frequently and thoroughly and give a suitable remedy. Most cases of mastitis clear up within a few days but some can make the cow very ill.

The first few milkings

The milk from the first few milkings is called colostrum – thick, yellow and full of antibodies, specially designed to start off the new calf. Do not drink it – give it to other calves or pigs.

From day four, the milk should be normal. The cow will soon build up to her peak yield, and you and she will settle into a regular daily routine. It is not essential always to milk at the same times, but cows are great time-keepers and expect you to be as well; you should space out your two milkings as close to twelve-hourly intervals as you can. If you have a day job, milk before and after work.

Goats

These are the stock to keep if you like goat's milk and want to operate on a smaller scale. Goats tend to be affectionate and obliging and seem to find the whole business of life rather fun. They are extremely sociable and relate closely to their human keepers, but unless you can be with her all the time do not keep just one as she really needs friends around her.

Breeds

The main dairy breeds are Toggenburg, Anglo-Nubian and Saanen. The Toggenburg is the smallest and the Saanen the biggest and highest yielding, while the Anglo-Nubian gives the richest milk. The British Saanen is the equivalent of the Holstein Friesian cow, so the smallholder is more likely to prefer the Anglo-Nubian. And then there are the Angoras and Cashmeres which you can keep for their coats, but are no good for milking.

Housing

This is very important for modern goats which cannot stay out like sheep and cattle and must be able to come in to a snug shed whenever it is cold or, especially, wet. If they have the run of a field with a shed in it, they can make their own decisions, but if they are tethered you must be prepared to get them in if it rains. Make sure they have a clean, dry bed. If you have to keep them in for any length of time, throw in some branches for them to chew.

Fencing

Not only are goats great escape artists, but they can cause havoc once out, ruining young trees, fruit bushes, vegetables or anything else they fancy. You must either lead them out and tether them or erect serious fences. There is a great deal to be said for tethering as you can choose exactly where to put them and make use of odd bits of grass and scrub, but it is labour-intensive and you must keep moving them on to clean ground. Ordinary netting or barbed wire fences are no use. Three or four strands of lively electric, with the top strand 1 m (3 ft 6 in) high, should stop them. The alternative is a chain link fence at least 1.2 m (4 ft) high with a strand of barbed wire above.

Feeding

Goats will eat just about anything, not only grass and all manner of shrubs, brambles and gorse but also vegetable waste and scraps. If they are milking well, up to 4.8 litres (8 pints) a day, they will need 1–2 kg (2–4 lb) per head of a concentrate ration and a similar amount of hay in winter. You could make this amount of hay by hand and stack it loose. The best way to store it is to build a floor above the goats' lying area and pitch the hay up on it. It will help to keep the goats warm and you can drop it down into a manger for feeding. Goats appreciate roots to eat in winter. Kids will need 1.2 litres (2 pints) milk a day for two or three months, and will move on to hay and a little concentrate, like calves.

Diseases

Goats are subject to worms and coccidiosis like sheep, and you should follow the same practices regarding clean grazing (see page 148). They can also get clostridial diseases and may need vaccinating, particularly against tetanus. Mastitis is not common, but infection can enter through damaged teats and needs swift treatment. Trim their feet regularly, and do not allow them to get fat, as they may get ketosis in late pregnancy and be unable to cope with the demands of the growing kids. Like cows and sheep, restrict their diet in early pregnancy but give some grain as they approach kidding and lactation.

Breeding and milking

Goats have to kid to milk (not as frequently as cows) and their lactations can last for over two years. Gestation is similar to sheep, so they do not have to be served until they have been in milk for a year or more. Hire or borrow a billy when you need him. Nannies should be dried off like cows eight weeks before kidding, which is usually quick and easy. Twins are normal and triplets not uncommon, though the first kidding usually produces one kid.

Milking goats is like milking cows but, as there are only two teats and not so much milk, it is easier. Goats' teats are usually ideally shaped for hand-milking. They are, however, a long way down so some people get the goats to skip up onto a stand to make it easier.

And, finally...

So there you have it – pigs, sheep, cattle or goats, or any combination of them – the choice is yours. In this brief guide to keeping them, we have tried to summarize some of the pleasures and pitfalls involved, but this is not comprehensive, and if you decide to go ahead, although you will learn rapidly 'on the hoof', you must be prepared to study further and pick up expert advice and assistance wherever you can.

Keeping bees

One of the most appealing aspects of gardening organically is the idea of the garden as a unified whole where nothing is wasted and where all the creatures contribute to its productivity. Bees are an important part of this process, and after you have been keeping them for a full year's cycle you will notice a big difference. Not only will you have a shelf full of jars of delicious golden honey but your fruit trees and bushes will bear a heavier crop, your vegetable garden will be more productive and your flowering plants will bloom for longer. Your neighbours will bless you because their gardens will benefit, too.

How do you start?

Many of us dream of owning an idyllic country garden with traditional white bee hives, sited in an old orchard, where bees hum peacefully among the lavender bushes. However, for many of us it begins and ends there.

Bees can appear frightening and the thought of stings, swarms and how much there is to learn about them puts many of us off keeping them. However, beekeeping is relatively simple and not at all frightening and it is well worth having a go. You don't even need a large country garden or an old orchard. Bees will live happily in small suburban gardens, even on city rooftops. As long as there are gardens and parks nearby where they can forage for nectar, they will make excellent honey.

Find a mentor – an experienced beekeeper who will show you what to do. It is easier to have an expert on hand than to learn it all from books. You need to be shown how to assemble the frames and the hive, how to use the tools and how to handle the bees. If you don't know any beekeepers, get in touch with your local beekeepers' association (in your Yellow Pages) and go along to a beginners' night. Many also run courses for beginners.

The beekeeper's tasks

- To encourage the bees to make honey and to store it in an accessible place.
- To discourage them from swarming.
- To help them survive the winter by feeding, medicating and keeping them warm.

Equipment

If you are going to keep bees, you will need some basic items of equipment. The following items are all you need to start off – others can be acquired later. You can buy all this stuff new from one of the suppliers of beekeeping equipment, but you can usually get it more cheaply, secondhand, through your local beekeepers' association. However, don't be tempted to economise by buying poor-quality items or old clothing or veils. When you are starting out you need to feel confident that the bees can't sting you.

Hives

There are two popular types of hive: the WBC and the National hive. The WBC hive is what most people visualize when they think of a hive – a traditional beehive, usually white, which looks pretty in the garden. For beginners, this is a good choice. The National hive looks like a square brown box and, because it is single-walled, is lighter and easier to move around than a WBC. This is the preferred choice of many experienced and professional beekeepers. Some of them think, however, that the double walls of the WBC help to keep the bees warm in winter and cool in summer.

Inside the hive

Inside the hive is the brood box, consisting of wooden frames suspended vertically on a frame with sheets of beeswax 'foundation' fastened into them with small tacks. The 'queen', or mother bee, who is really just an egg-laying machine, lives in the brood box. The worker bees build onto, or 'draw out', the foundation with their own wax to form cells in which the queen lays eggs. The workers also store pollen and honey in some of the cells.

Above the brood box is the 'queen excluder': a perforated sheet of metal with holes large enough for the workers to pass through but insufficiently large for the queen to enter.

Above the queen excluder you can put one or more 'supers'. These are not so high as the brood box but otherwise identical. The worker bees draw out the wax foundation and store pollen and honey in the cells but, as the queen cannot get in, frames of honey can be taken off without damaging eggs or grubs or, worse, inadvertently injuring or removing the queen.

Above the super is a wooden or glass 'crown board', which has an oval hole for the bees to enter, and above that goes the roof of the hive.

Clothing

You will also need good protective clothing, including the following items:
● An all-in-one boiler suit, ideally with an integral hood and visor (or you can have a separate helmet or hat and veil).
● Some sturdy rubber boots in which to tuck the legs of the suit.
● Long fine gloves of rubber or leather.

All these should, if possible, be white. Bees are very sensitive to colour, preferring flowers in certain colours, and they find white the most neutral and soothing. If you are in white, they will be calm and less likely to sting.

Smokers

A smoker is essential. Smoke puffed into the hive makes the bees drowsy and easy to handle. This is not because they are anaesthetized by the smoke; on the contrary, the presence of smoke alerts the bees to danger and they rush to their honey stores and fill themselves with food in preparation for an emergency. All this takes only about three minutes.

Puff some smoke into the hive entrance, wait for a few moments, then start opening the hive. By this time, the bees will be sleepy, full of food and less likely to sting. While you work on the hive, you may need to give a few more puffs of smoke occasionally.

The smoker is just a small firebox with a spout and a squeezing mechanism which draws air over the fuel and produces plenty of cool smoke. Lighting the smoker and keeping it alight needs a bit of practice. Hessian sacking cut into strips is the best fuel as it burns for a long time, but you can use hay or dry lawn mowings, or even buy an aerosol spray that smells of smoke and is much easier to use.

Hive tools

The other piece of equipment you will need is a hive tool. This is a flat piece of rigid metal with a curved end, which you will use for moving and removing frames within the hive.

Handling bees

Now you are ready for the bees! You can start with a swarm, but this is an unreliable source and you won't know the temperament of the bees. The best way is to acquire a nuclear colony from an experienced beekeeper.

This consists of a frame containing worker bees and cells of eggs and developing grubs, and a queen. They can be from a named strain, such as New Zealand bees, which are a pretty pale gold colour and particularly gentle.

Stings

A word about stings before you get going. Have you ever been stung by a honey bee? You need to know whether you have an allergic reaction to the venom. It is quite rare, but if you do, go no further. Any more stings will make the problem worse and you will need to take precautions against anaphylactic shock.

The thought of being stung is what puts most people off keeping bees and can make beginners very nervous when working on the hive. However, if you have good protective clothing, you will rarely be stung and this will give you the confidence to handle bees calmly and the bees themselves will be less likely to sting. Talking to them quietly can help, too.

Dealing with stings

If you are unlucky enough to be stung the most important thing is to remove the venom immediately. Do this with a clean blade – a pocket or kitchen knife is best but many people use their hive tool. You will see the small pink entry mark on your skin. Scrape the blade towards this point until the sting pops out and repeat several times to make sure it's all out. Rub on a little antihistamine cream to soothe any remaining soreness, but in an hour or two this will have gone. If you are stung on the face or inside your mouth, remove the sting immediately but also go to your doctor for antihistamine tablets or an injection.

Keeping notes

Keep a record of all that you do to your hives and when you do it. You can learn a lot from looking back over your beekeeping activities during the previous year. If you have several hives, you need to know when a super was put on or a queen replaced. Most beekeepers put a postcard inside the hive on the crown board and write down what they have done before closing the hive. However, the bees may eat the edges of the card, it's difficult to write legibly while wearing gloves, and there may not be enough space to write what you want. Keep a special notebook for recording your beekeeping activities. Write up your notes as soon as you have finished with the hives or you will forget something important. If you have several hives, you need to number them and keep separate notes on each.

The beekeeper's year

Throughout the year you will have to perform different tasks. Here is a guide to what you will have to do on a seasonal basis.

Spring

Some time around mid-February there comes a day when spring seems almost here. There is some warmth in the sun, the birds are singing and snowdrops, aconites and crocuses are blooming in sheltered parts of the garden. You may even see a honey bee and rush to look at the hives. Bees are flying in and out, enjoying the sunshine and getting busy – they have survived the winter.

Now is the time to refill their feeder with sugar syrup in order to give them some easily accessible food. There is very little nectar about at this time of year and their stock of honey will be low. Leave the covering over the hive and do not open it until the weather is much warmer, probably at the end of March.

Preparing the hive

For the new beekeeper, now is the time to start your colony. If you have bought a new bee hive you can set it up straight away. If it is second-hand, however, it may need cleaning and repairing. You can use a blow torch and a paint scraper on all the internal parts of the hive. This will help to destroy any disease as well as removing old wax and propolis, the sticky bee glue. If it is a white WBC hive you will want to repaint the white exterior and possibly recover the roof.

Siting the hive

Decide where you are going to position your hive. It should, if possible, be in a warm sheltered site facing south and not overhung with trees. The bees need a clear flight path into the hive entrance so don't put it opposite a high wall or building, nor where the bees will have to cross your neighbour's garden. It is a good idea to build a brick platform on which to stand the hive. This will prevent the base rotting, help to keep the area free from weeds and make a dry place for you to stand on when you are working on the hive. Make your platform big enough for two hives – you may want to expand.

Stocking the hive

When the nuclear colony arrives, place the frame containing the worker bees and brood, i.e. the eggs and developing grubs, in the centre of the brood box. The queen arrives separately so have a good look at her before she goes into the hive – this will help you to recognise her later. She is larger than the workers, a long elegant shape with a more pointed rear end. She has a sting but uses it only on another queen. To make it easier to spot her, the queen can be marked with a coloured dot on her head with a felt tip pen. Change the colour each year so that her age is obvious.

Put the queen in a small plastic container, closing its entrance with a boiled sweet. Place in the centre of the brood chamber. The workers will eat their way through the sweet, and by the time the queen is released they will be used to her smell and will accept her as their queen. She will start to lay eggs immediately.

Checking on the hive

From now on you need to go through the hive once a week. This must be done regularly from about mid-April onwards, when the honey is starting to be produced, until autumn, when the hive is closed up for the winter. Do it on the same day each week to establish a routine or the days will slip by and you will realize that you have not inspected the hive for two or three weeks. This is when trouble can start. However, if it is very cold, windy or raining, do not open the hive; postpone it until the next day. Neither you nor the bees will enjoy it.

Put on all your protective clothing, making sure there are no gaps at the neck, wrists or ankles. Light the smoker, getting it well alight and puffing air through it so that it doesn't go out while you are carrying out the examination. Approaching the hive from the side to avoid crossing the bees' flight path, puff some smoke into the entrance and wait for about three minutes for it to take effect. Then, working slowly and calmly, remove the roof and several of the lifts, piling them neatly to one side. Run your hive tool under the edge of the crown board and remove it gently. Next examine the underside to ensure the queen is not there and lean it beside the hive entrance. Any bees clinging to it will return to the hive. Puff a little more smoke into the top of the hive to send the bees down into the brood chamber.

Starting at one end, insert the curved edge of the hive tool under the first frame to loosen it and push it away from the next frame. Lift out the frame and, holding it by the lugs, examine each side, keeping the frame vertical at all times. (A full frame of honey can fall apart if horizontal.) Put the first frame by the hive entrance with the crown board and, using the space this leaves, work through the hive from end to end, examining each frame and replacing them in the same order.

The outside frames will often be empty. As you get nearer the centre you will see cells filled with honey and capped with wax and some still uncapped. There may be cells filled with yellow or brown pollen. On the inner frames you will see a pattern of sealed and unsealed brood, the developing grubs. There will also be what seem to be empty cells, but look carefully and you will see thread-like white eggs laid by the queen. They are upright when newly laid, then turn on their side. A worker bee is in egg form for three days, in larva form for five, then the cell is capped with wax. After another 13 days, the egg hatches and the young bee emerges from its cell.

At the edges of the outer combs of the brood nest you may see cells with domed wax caps. These contain drone larvae. They are sealed on the tenth day and emerge on the twenty-fourth. Drones are bigger and squarer than workers, and their duty is to impregnate a young queen – they do no other work and have no sting. Somewhere near the centre of the brood nest, near where eggs have been laid, you may see the queen, easily spotted if she is marked, although she may be hidden under a mass of workers. Gently move them with your finger or blow on them to reveal the queen. Beginners are always reassured to see the queen and hunt for her avidly but this is unnecessary. If there are freshly laid eggs, you know that she has been there very recently.

It is more important to search for queen cells. These are quite distinctive: longer than ordinary cells of brood, and pointed, but the bees build them in safe places – hidden corners where they are difficult to see. When empty they are called queen cups. The bees build them in readiness, particularly if the hive is getting overcrowded and they are preparing to swarm. They are a warning of impending trouble and must be destroyed by squashing them with the hive tool. Make sure you have found and eradicated them all. If you find one or more with queen larvae inside it is even more important to destroy them, unless you want the colony to supercede, i.e. replace the old queen with a young one.

If you inspect the hive regularly you should be able to avert any trouble before the bees even think of swarming. As soon as the outer frames of the brood box are beginning to fill up, either with brood or stored honey, you should put on a 'super'. This is a shallower box of frames which is placed on top of the brood box, separated by a queen excluder. The queen continues to lay eggs in the brood box but the workers can store honey in the super, making it easy for you to remove it without disturbing or injuring the queen.

Summer

Hot, drowsy summer days when beekeepers talk rapturously of the flow of honey, and you will soon learn to recognize the signs of it. Many bees fly determinedly in and out of the hive and the supers fill up fast. Do not remove a super until the cells have been capped, but if it is nearly full you should add another, or even two if you have a strong colony.

Early summer honey

If you have over-wintered a colony and it has built up numbers early in the year you should get some honey in early summer. If you are surrounded by fields of bright yellow rape the bees will head for this and you will get a lot of pale, rather bland honey. If you are lucky, your bees will have foraged in orchards and gardens and produce a little of the pale gold, flowery-tasting honey from the spring blossoms.

Swarming

The early summer months are the busiest time for the beekeeper. Hives must be examined weekly, supers removed or added as necessary and queen cups and cells destroyed. The colony is multiplying fast as the queen can lay up to 2,000 eggs in a day, and you will notice many more bees in the garden and the hive. This is the time when bees are most likely to swarm; they do this if the hive is overcrowded. The queen and half or more of the colony leave the hive and look for a new home. The first sign will be the sound and sight of many bees flying round the garden. The buzzing noise sounds angry and frightening. Scout bees will search for a good site for the new home – an empty hive, a corner of a barn or even a dead tree trunk. Once they have found somewhere, the swarm will assemble in a dark mass of bees, the size and shape of a rugby football, with the queen somewhere in the centre, and they will fly to their new home.

If you have never dealt with a swarm before, you should try to get someone who is experienced to help you. Don't be frightened; swarming bees do not sting – they are much too preoccupied. All the same, you should put on all your protective clothing.

If the swarm has disappeared, search the garden and surrounding area. Take an empty skep if you have one, or a sturdy cardboard box, and an old sheet. When you find the swarm it will probably be suspended from the branch of a tree. Hold the skep or box under the swarm and give the branch a sharp tap. The swarm should drop into the box which you then cover with the sheet. Leave the bees in the box for several hours to settle.

If you are well-prepared, you will have an empty hive ready. Carry the skep to the hive in a wheelbarrow. You will need a piece of wood as wide as the hive and long enough to make a gentle slope between the ground and the hive entrance. Prop this firmly under the entrance, uncover the skep, spreading the sheet on the ground, and shake the bees on to the sheet. They will start to run up the slope into their new home. You will need to feed the new colony with sugar syrup, about a gallon, over the first week or until they have built up their own stores of honey.

Dealing with the old hive

You are now left with a small colony of bees in your original hive, with no queen. Light your smoker and smoke the hive. Open it and then work methodically through the frames, destroying all but one of the queen cells. Choose one with a queen larva in it. You will notice that bees in a queenless hive behave strangely. They move in an aimless and rather anxious way and make a louder buzzing sound. They just don't seem contented. The new queen will hatch in 25 days. At least five days after that, on a hot still day, she will fly from the hive and mate with several drones. She will then return to the hive and in another five days will start to lay eggs. Her brief youth is over and for the rest of her life she will do nothing but lay eggs. The size of the colony will drop before it starts to increase again, and honey production will be reduced.

Signs of swarming

If you have no spare hive you will have to ask a neighbouring beekeeper to take the swarm away and hive it. This is sad as you have now lost half your bees and won't have such a big crop of honey, so avoid swarming by watching out for the warning signs. These are:

● **Overcrowding**: If all but two frames in the brood box are full, put on a super. If the super is filling fast, put on another.
● **Queen cells**: Keep a careful watch and destroy them.

Autumn

This is the most rewarding time of year for the beekeeper and you can relax a bit. On warm September days the bees are still working on late flowers but they won't swarm now so there is less urgency about going through the hive. In late summer or early autumn comes the moment when you can extract the honey. When the super is full and most or all of the cells have been capped is the best time, but some people say it's easier, albeit messier, to extract honey from uncapped cells.

Extracting the honey

The day before you plan to take off the honey put an extra crown board between the brood box and the super, fitted with a bee escape. This is a one-way door so the bees can go down into the brood chamber but not back into the super. By the next day most of them will be in the brood chamber. Decide on where to do the extracting – a room with a washable floor is essential – and assemble the equipment. The most important thing is the extractor.

There are various types and sizes. Electrically operated ones are physically easier to use but they can be heavy to lift. Some have integral heaters – useful for rape honey which sets very quickly when cold. One of the best is a simple electric extractor which holds two frames of honey. Made of plastic, it is light, fairly shallow and easy to clean. However, if you have several hives, you will need a bigger one.

All extractors work on the same principle: frames of honey are fastened into a drum that rotates like a spin-dryer throwing the honey outwards. It runs down the sides and collects at the base, where a tap drains it off.

In addition, you will need a holding tank which has several filters of increasingly fine mesh, a piece of muslin or nylon net, an uncapping knife or serrated bread knife, jars and labels.

When you are ready to extract the honey, put on your protective clothing and light your smoker. Take a wheelbarrow, a large washable tray and a soft hand brush out to the hive. Smoke the hive as usual and remove the roof, crownboard and lifts. Starting at one end of the super, remove each frame. Shake and brush off any remaining bees, dropping them back into the hive. Put each cleared frame on the tray in the wheelbarrow. Reassemble the hive and leave the frames in a warm place overnight.

Take as many frames as will fit into your extractor and slice off the wax cappings with a knife. Fit them into the extractor and turn it on. You will hear honey and wax splatter against the extractor walls. Remove the empty frames and replace with full ones until all the honey is extracted. Put the empty frames outside near the hive and let the bees clean them up.

When all the honey has collected in the base, you can move the extractor on to a table and position the holding tank underneath. Tie some muslin loosely over the top and then turn on the extractor tap. Leave the honey to drip through for about 24 hours. Put the wax cappings in a sieve and add any wax from the muslin or filters. Leave the honey in the tank for a day to clear and settle, and then draw it off into clean jars. Put on the lids, wipe the jars and label them.

Beeswax

The beeswax can be washed and re-used. Tip the contents of the sieve into a bucket and cover with cold water. When the honey has dissolved, tip the clean wax back into the sieve and leave to drain. Then melt it in an old saucepan over a very gentle heat and pour the liquid wax through some muslin into a basin or tin. When it has cooled, you will have a small block of pure beeswax .

Feeding the bees

You will need to feed the bees as you have removed their winter store of food. You can use a special plastic feeder or an upturned jar with a perforated lid. Make up a strong sugar solution by measuring 1 kg (2.2 lb) granulated sugar into a large bowl and pouring over it 500 ml (18 fl oz) boiling water. Stir until the sugar has dissolved and then leave until cold.

Pour the syrup into the feeder and check it once every two to three days, refilling it when empty. The bees may take up to 4.8 litres (8 pints) of syrup, converting it into a simple kind of honey and then storing it and capping it as they do flower honey.

Guarding against varroa mite

Autumn is also the time to put medicated strips of plastic into the hive to kill the dreaded varroa mite. This is a small parasitic insect which lives on bees, weakening them and ultimately destroying the whole colony. You should suspend two strips in the brood chamber between the frames of brood and remove them after six weeks.

Winter

This is the quiet time of the year for beekeepers and bees alike. During the last warm days of autumn, the bees forage for any nectar they can find; then, as the days turn colder, they remain in the hive. The drones are expelled to die of cold outside; their useful life is over and the foodstore must be husbanded for the queen and workers. The remaining colony forms a dense spherical mass in the centre of the hive, close to their stores of honey so they can feed quickly without losing heat. There they will stay until the first warm days of spring.

Helping bees survive the winter

There are several things that you can do to help your bees to survive the winter. Begin by narrowing the hive entrance with blocks of wood, slipped in on each side of the opening to leave just a small hole. Insert a strip of perforated metal behind the blocks. This will keep out mice, who will try to enter the hive when the bees are quiescent and steal the honey. You can also put a folded piece of blanket inside the hive to keep the cold out. After the bees are put to bed you must leave them undisturbed until the spring. Do not open the hive when the weather is cold as bees can get chilled very quickly.

Looking after equipment

Winter is the best time to repair and overhaul your beekeeping equipment. Put aside some time to clean it up and repaint any spare hives. You can also order any new equipment that you will need for the coming season.

part 3

the organic home

Natural health and beauty

When most of us decide to 'go organic', we start with what we put in our mouths and grow in our gardens. However, we should also consider what we put on our skin, hair and body. It is illogical to screen out chemicals from what we eat but to slap them on from top-to-toe instead. If you care not only about your own health but also that of the environment, it makes sense to look for cosmetics that are sustainably produced from renewable sources. In your quest for holistic health, there are plenty of simple, natural remedies that you can make yourself at home, using the fruit, vegetables and herbs that you have cultivated organically.

Organic beauty products

There is an increasingly wide selection of truly organic cosmetics on the market, and The Soil Association has standards for health and beauty care, which means that you can look for their familiar symbol on packaging.

To carry the Soil Association symbol, products must be at least 75 per cent organic, in which case they can say 'Made With Organic…' on the front of the packaging, or 95 per cent or over, in which case they can be labelled 'Organic'. Organic ingredients must be used if they are available on the market anywhere.

What is more, there is an incredibly long list of forbidden ingredients, including many foaming agents, emulsifiers and preservatives. Currently, this means that the overall selection of products may be more limited than you're used to, while manufacturers scratch their heads and get on with working out new ways to make shampoo froth or preserve products without using chemicals that currently have a health question mark over them.

So you will discover balms, oils, cleansers, moisturizers and body creams, bath 'teas', soap and hair conditioner – but you are less likely to find a truly organic shampoo. For more information on which ranges are the most natural, turn to page 205.

It is also likely to be some time before we see certified organic make-up. If you want to be a truly natural beauty, you should check out the ranges that use mineral pigments rather than chemical colourants or those derived from coal tar, some of which are recognized as being carcinogenic, albeit when applied or ingested in much larger quantities than you will find in a lipstick or eyeshadow.

Read the labels

If the label boldly states that the product is organic, or has organic ingredients, but does not carry the symbol (or a European equivalent, for instance from Ecocert), its organicness might be just marketing spin. As yet, there is no legal definition for organic cosmetics, as there is for food. That will hopefully come in the next few years, but, meanwhile, beauty companies that do not carry the symbol can still, alas, hype their 'organic-ness' as much as they like. The symbol is a short-cut – if it is there, you can totally trust the product's organic credentials; if it's not, it is up to you to make up your mind how much you trust the manufacturer to be honest.

Making your cosmetics

To be totally 100 per cent reassured by what you put on your skin, hair and body, you might want to think about making your own cosmetics. This is much easier than it sounds. There was a real trend for home-made cosmetics in the 1970s, and most teenagers have experimented with banana face masks, or slathering yoghurt on their faces. But, once again, women (and even some men!) are discovering that it is possible to make high-quality, effective products at home, using simple ingredients – some of them from your kitchen store cupboard and others sourced from reputable companies (see page 205), which offer a full range of herbs, oils, beeswax and other essentials by mail order.

Organic guidelines

The following guidelines will not only help you to make organic beauty choices but also to reduce the number of beauty products that you use regularly every day.

● To moisturize your body, try switching to oils, perhaps those infused with aromatherapeutic essential oils, which do not require chemical preservatives. If you are not accustomed to using oils – on the face and/or body – then you may be surprised to discover just how quickly they sink into the skin.

● You can have fun experimenting with making your own cosmetics at home, using fresh organic ingredients (see page 176).

● It's a simple rule of thumb that those beauty products with short ingredients lists tend to be purer and more natural than those that feature a long string of chemicals with unpronounceable names starting with para-, oxy-, benzo-, methyl-, etc. Although it is European law that all cosmetics must be labelled in Latin (which, frankly, makes everything sound like a chemical!), many natural beauty companies offer the English translation after the Latin name on the labels on their products. In fact, the Soil Association rules for organic health and beauty care require this.

● Get into a dialogue with the beauty companies you buy from – you can often do this via their website (which is usually listed on the packaging). If their products do not carry the symbol and you are not sure of the manufacturer's integrity, or you are confused by the ingredients listed, you can write and ask them whether they use petrochemical ingredients, or what their policy is on Genetically Modified Organisms. In Europe, where we made a lot of noise about GM early on, many manufacturers swiftly scrambled to find GM-free ingredients, but in America, this has been less of a concern.

What you need

Cut down on the number of products you use. Most of us use at least 30 beauty products over an average day and have an unnecessary 'armoury' of them, which can lead to skin 'overload' – one reason why so many of us (63 per cent, according to some studies) complain we have sensitive skin. Most women will need the following beauty items:
● Cleanser
● Something for removing eye make-up (a good, balm-style cleanser will do that, too)
● Moisturizer and/or facial oil
● Body cream or oil
● Deodorant
● Shampoo and (probably) conditioner
● Toothpaste
● Whatever make-up you consider 'essential'

Be a natural beauty

It is really surprisingly simple to make your own skincare and bodycare products and, in reality, making your own beauty treats is the only way you can be 100 per cent certain of what you are putting on your skin.

If you care about the food on your plate, the next logical step is to start thinking carefully about the products that you rely on to nourish your body from without – because our skin is actually highly absorbent. In fact, according to experts like Rob McCaleb of the Herb Research Foundation in the United States, up to 60 per cent of what we put on our skins ends up in our bloodstream.

By making your own beauty products at home, you are also harnessing the maximum plant power from what you put on your face, skin or hair – it's fresher, and more potent, too, as a result. You will also save money as many of the basic ingredients for the products that are featured in the following pages are actually store cupboard staples which cost very little indeed.

Shelf life

You will have to change your expectations slightly, however, if you are going to make your own beauty products. Commercial cosmetics contain lots of preservatives, because they are designed to withstand the most irresponsible use, such as keeping them in steamy bathrooms, leaving lids off jars, scooping out gunk with less-than-clean hands (and leaving dirt and germs behind in the moisturizer, cleanser or body cream).

The beauty products that you will make yourself at home will not last as long as the products you buy, and therefore if you make them from fresh ingredients, you will need to do so often and use them quite quickly.

You will have to use your nose – and your common sense. If something smells 'off', or

goes a funny colour, or separates or otherwise changes in texture, you must throw it out and then start all over again. After all, you would not think of keeping, say, a Hollandaise sauce for three months and expect it to stay fresh all that time, would you? So, really, all that is needed is a simple change of mind-set.

In reality, however, many home-made beauty products – especially if they are based just on oil or oil/beeswax – do keep for six months, at least, before spoiling.

Sensitivity

It is very important to do a 'patch test' (right) on your skin before slapping a home-made beauty product all over you. Actually, it is sensible to do this test with all store-bought cosmetics, too, but few of us bother. We can be sensitive to some natural ingredients just as we can be to synthetic chemicals. Think about it: nettles and poison ivy are natural, but they will trigger immediate skin reactions.

Individually, we may be sensitive to a whole range of other natural ingredients, such as avocado oil, essential oils, glycerine, lanolin,

Doing a patch test

● Apply a small amount of the beauty cosmetic that you have made on your inner arm, immediately below the elbow.
● Cover with sticking plaster (unless you are allergic to plaster) and then leave for 24 hours.
● Alternatively, you can apply the cream behind one ear.
● If you experience any soreness, redness or irritation, then your skin is reacting to an ingredient, which could well be one of those listed below, and therefore you should avoid using the product on a wider scale.

simple tincture of benzoin, sweet almond oil and wheatgerm oil. If you know that your skin is sensitive and touchy, it is worth carrying out a patch test (see above) before applying any creams that you have made or bought to your face or large areas of the body.

Note: Never use home-made treatments on abrasions, acne or breakouts – they could inflame them and make them worse.

Skincare basics

Here are some simple recipes for a very easy but effective skincare regime.

Geranium and rose moisturizer

This recipe is for normal-to-dry and sensitive skins, and it can be used after cleansing in the morning or at night. It has a wonderful smooth texture and a pretty rose fragrance. Rose is renowned for its anti-ageing powers, so you may find that it even helps defy the march of time, too.

- *5 g (1 teaspoon) cocoa butter*
- *5 g (1 teaspoon) beeswax (grated or granules)*
- *30 ml (1 fl oz) grapeseed oil*
- *15 ml (1 tablespoon) apricot kernel oil*
- *30 ml (1 fl oz) rose petal infusion (see page 186 for how to make an infusion)*
- *15 ml (1 tablespoon) glycerine*
- *5 drops rose essential oil*
- *5 drops geranium essential oil*

1 Heat the cocoa butter and the beeswax in the oils in a double boiler or a bowl set over a saucepan of boiling water.

2 When these are dissolved, remove from the heat, allow to cool slightly and slowly drizzle in the glycerine and the rose infusion, beating all the time with a hand whisk or electric hand blender until the texture is really creamy and super smooth.

3 Lastly, whizz in the essential oils and transfer to a sterilized jar. This will keep in the fridge for around two months, or about one month in normal 'bathroom conditions'.

Oil-free moisturizer

This recipe is for oilier and problem skins.

- *20 g (³/₄ oz) linseeds*
- *200 ml (7 fl oz) boiling purified, mineral or tap water*
- *15 ml (1 tablespoon) glycerine*
- *15 ml (1 tablespoon) rosewater*
- *2 drops neroli essential oil*
- *2 drops lemon essential oil*

1 Crack the linseeds open to release their goodness in a blender or coffee grinder, for a few seconds.

2 Transfer to a small bowl or cup and pour the boiling water over the seeds. Stir continuously while the mixture cools down. Strain off the linseeds and compost them, if you can, to ensure that nothing goes to waste.

3 Mix the linseed liquid, which will have become quite gel-like, with the glycerine and rosewater to form a lightly moisturizing lotion. Pour into a sterilized bottle with a wide neck, add the essential oils, and shake. Apply to cleansed skin, morning and evening. This will keep for a fortnight or so.

Cucumber facial toner

Splash blended cucumber pulp over your face as a cleansing and refreshing toner.

- *20 cm (8 in) chunk of cucumber*

1 Whizz the cucumber in a food processor or blender until it is liquid.

2 Strain the liquid into a sterilized bottle and keep in the fridge – it will be ultra-refreshing. Cucumbers are packed with vitamin C.

Simple cleansing cream

This cream melts away make-up and grime as effectively as any commercial cleanser but is best used with a muslin washcloth or a face flannel and hot water. Customize it to your complexion type by varying the infusion (or 'tea') that makes up the liquid element of this creamy cleanser. You can make: rosemary tea for problem skins prone to breakouts; chamomile tea for normal skins; marigold tea for sensitive skins. To find out how to make these teas, turn to page 186.

- 5 g (¹/₄ oz) beeswax
- 100 ml (3¹/₂ fl oz) grapeseed oil
- ¹/₂ teaspoon borax
- 150 ml (¹/₄ pint) of your chosen infusion (see above)
- 20 drops of essential oil to match your infusion (chamomile for normal skins; marigold for sensitive skins; rosemary for problem skins)

1 Place the beeswax and the grapeseed oil in a double boiler or 'bain marie', or a bowl suspended over a saucepan of boiling water, and then stir gently until the wax has disappeared into the oil completely.

2 Remove the bowl containing the beeswax and grapeseed oil from the heat and then set aside and allow to cool for 5 minutes.

3 Dissolve the borax in your chosen infusion (see page 186), which should have cooled to around body temperature.

4 Pour the wax/oil mixture into a bowl and add the tea/borax mixture, a little at a time, beating with a hand-held mixer until the consistency is creamy and thick. This will take around 5 minutes.

5 Add the essential oils and stir to blend thoroughly, before transferring to a sterilized jar. This will keep in the fridge for around two months, or about one month in normal 'bathroom conditions'.

Beauty tips

- Skincare professionals say they can always spot when someone's drinking adequate water. Ideally, you should drink 2.5 litres (4 pints) a day of mineral or filtered tap water. Keeping a large bottle on your desk helps you keep tabs on how much you are drinking.
- Exercise is one of the best free beauty treatments around. Get out in the fresh air, have a 20-minute brisk walk – and you won't need blusher. Walking delivers oxygen to the skin more effectively than an 'oxygen facial' ever can.
- Having a beauty emergency? Gone away without your sponge bag? Olive oil is one of the best beauty treatments that nature has to offer. At a pinch, it can be used to dissolve make-up, or as a body moisturizer (massaged into the skin), or even a drop or two on the face, as a night treatment, to leave your skin feeling gloriously supple.
- Prevention is better than cure when it comes to anti-ageing. From April to October, wear a skin cream with SPF15. To be a natural beauty, avoid synthetic chemical sunscreens and look for products that block the sun's rays with titanium dioxide or zinc oxide.

Special skin treats

Name	Preperation	Application	Benefits
Nourishing avocado face mask	Mix one teaspoon of honey with a few tablespoons of avocado and mash until creamy.	Massage into the skin and leave on for around 5 minutes; rinse, then moisturise.	The fatty acids, protein and vitamins A and C are extremely hydrating for dry skins.
Strawberry cleansing mask	Mix one mashed strawberry with a teaspoon of honey, a tablespoon of yoghurt and a tiny squeeze of lemon juice.	Mix and apply to the face; leave on for 15 minutes and rinse, then moisturize the skin.	Be warned: sensitive skins can react to strawberries. Masks should be applied to skin that has already been cleansed.
Potato skin soother	Peel and mash 2 potatoes (which act as a natural skin-soother), and add one egg yolk (to moisturize) and 2 tablespoons of milk (to cleanse).	Spread on and relax for 15 minutes before rinsing off.	Your skin will be fresher-looking – and calm!
Refreshing facial spray	Take 2 heaped teaspoons each of fresh mint and dill, and a teaspoon of fresh parsley and pour 85 ml (3 fl oz) boiled mineral or purified tap water over the herbs, to make an infusion (see page 186).	Strain and pour into a bottle with a spray atomizer, and mist as required.	This is lovely in hot weather, especially for dry skin. If your skin tends to greasiness, replace the water with witch hazel, which has an astringent action. This keeps for a couple of days in the fridge.
Chamomile foot tea	Start by boiling around 4 litres (14 pints) of water in a large stockpot. Next add around 115 g (4 oz) of dried chamomile flowers. Cover and steep for around 10–20 minutes; strain and cool until comfortable to the touch.	Pour into a basin and soak your feet for at least 10 minutes.	A footbath is a wonderful winter treat for your feet, and the rest of your body will benefit from chamomile's soothing properties, as the herbs are absorbed through your skin and into your bloodstream.
Tub tea	Nothing could be easier than creating a bath from your favourite herbal tea blend. You can either use a large metal 'tea ball', or you can pile the herbs onto a piece of muslin, approximately 30 cm (12 in) square. Use a total of around 50 g (2 oz) of herbs per bag. Secure it into a 'parcel' with a length of raffia or ribbon.	Dangle from the taps so that the water can rush through the herbs while you are filling the bath, then take the bag off the taps and soak in the water while you do the same. Squeeze the herb 'parcel' to extract the maximum goodness from it.	Choose herbs that you would like to have the desired effect, from the following list: **Stimulating**: rosemary, peppermint; **Refreshing**: basil, lemon balm, mint **Cleansing**: thyme, sage, lemon balm **Invigorating**: bay, raspberry leaves **Relaxing**: chamomile, elderflower, lavender.
Sugar hand softener	You need 25 g (1 oz) organic sugar, and 30 ml (2 tablespoons) of organic olive oil. Add a drop or two of your favourite essential oil (sweet orange is lovely). Now combine the ingredients in a small bowl	With your fingers, gently massage the mixture into your hands. Use a hot towel and warm water to remove the mixture, then dry your hands and apply your favourite natural hand cream.	Hands that have become chapped and red over the winter respond wonderfully to a sugar scrub. The tiny grains make an excellent exfoliator, and olive oil softens roughness. It is particularly effective for rough knuckles and around the cuticles.

Organic health

There are some simple steps that we can all take in our everyday lives to increase our organic health. If you follow these guidelines, you will not only feel healthier and more energized but also help to prevent a wide range of common health problems and diseases.

Get more sleep

This is the best way of all to repair, restore and re-energize your body – and fight infections. How often have you gone down with a cold or 'flu after burning the candle at both ends? In a frantic world, we often deprive ourselves of the rest needed to help our bodies stay naturally healthy.

Complementary therapies

Instead of rushing to your family doctor with every itch, headache or cough, experiment with complementary therapies and identify those that work best for you. We are all different, and whereas homeopathy might be highly effective for one person it might be useless for someone else, who might find that reflexology delivers amazing benefits. Real health is not just the absence of illness – it's a feeling of wellbeing and energy.

Stay active

Exercise for 30 minutes at least four times a week to get your heart and lungs pumping aerobically. Choose an exercise you enjoy, such as swimming, cycling, dance or even walking – often described as 'nature's best medicine' and the easiest to incorporate into daily life. Leave the car behind and walk from A to B more often. Remember that it is very important that you like the exercise you choose or you will not stick to it. You should try to do some form of stretching exercise also to maintain your flexibility, like yoga or Pilates.

Eat a healthy diet

Eat as healthy and varied a diet as you can, aiming for a minimum of five servings of (organically-grown) fruit and vegetables a day, but make sure at least two of these are vegetables. And, no, potato crisps do not count as a serving of vegetables! Ideally, look for the vegetables that are high in health-boosting antioxidants: the yellow, red and dark green vegetables, such as tomatoes, squash, spinach and carrots, etc.

Cut down on sugar

Too much sugar lowers our natural immunity. That does not mean, of course, that you cannot enjoy an occasional sweet treat, but many people fuel themselves with sugar-rich foods for an instant boost – and then they have to eat something sweet again, when their energy slumps later. If this applies to you, try to break this sugar cycle.

Simple herbal medicine

The tradition of growing medicinal herbs goes back far into the mists of time. For thousands of years, people have turned to plant wisdom to treat and prevent disease, keep food safe and fresh – and simply to make life more colourful, through clothing dyes and pigments.

If you have even the tiniest space outdoors, it is possible to grow your own remedies. In fact, many herbs are so easy to cultivate that they practically grow themselves. The perfect place for a 'medicinal garden' is right outside your back door, where you can grab a handful of herbs not just for cooking, but when you are feeling under the weather. Many herbs thrive on benign neglect: the less water they get, the stronger their medicinal compounds. And, in most cases, there is no need to feed them, either. Here are some basic 'home-grown remedies', along with details of how to grow them and how to transform them into your aromatic helpers.

WARNING: Do not take herbs if you are pregnant (or planning to get pregnant soon), breastfeeding, or taking pharmaceutical drugs, without speaking to your doctor first.

Aloe vera *(Aloe vera)*
Even if you do not have a space outdoors, you can successfully grow an aloe vera plant; a kitchen windowsill is an ideal spot for this spiky plant. Slice open the leaves and they reveal a gel-like sap which is useful for healing burns, cuts and blemishes. A native of Africa, aloe vera will grow happily in much cooler climates, provided it has plenty of drainage (add some grit to the compost, if you like),

and has a sunny spot. If you live where there is a risk of frost, aloe vera needs to be brought in for protection during the winter, as freezing temperatures will kill it.

Although it looks like a succulent, aloe is related to the lily plant and needs plenty of water. You can harvest the leaves all year round: cut off a spike, as required, and separate the soothing, cooling, healing gel from the green outer skin. It is also said to help eczema and fungal infections, such as ringworm.

Echinacea *(Echinacea spp.)*

Echinacea, also known as purple cone flower, was one of the most important herbs used by Native American Indian healers. It has anti-bacterial, anti-fungal and anti-viral properties and, today, many people swear by echinacea's immune-boosting power to keep them free from colds during the winter.

The purple flowers, which appear in late summer, look architectural in a mixed flower border – the plant grows up to 1.2 m (4 ft) in height. Echinacea prefers fertile, well-drained soil and a sunny position.

There are some excellent commercial echinacea products on the market, but you can also make your own echinacea tea. You should harvest in autumn, when the plant has died back, and use the roots to make a decoction (see page 186).

Fennel *(Feniculum offinalis)*

It is no coincidence that Indian restaurants set out tiny dishes of fennel seeds to chew on after dinner: it is excellent for wind, indigestion or colic. Fennel tea is a terrific 'after drink' (also available in easy-to-use tea bags). The ancient Roman scientist Pliny the Elder listed 22 medical uses for fennel. The essential oil, for instance, can be added to external rubs for bronchial problems, whereas fennel is a good mouth-wash for gum disease and sore throats.

Fennel grows easily from seed and, once you have got it, it will seed itself. It loves full sun and rich, dry soil. Gather the seeds from

the end of the feathery stalks; they can be used fresh or dry. Crush one or two teaspoons with a pestle and mortar and then steep in a cup of boiling water. The fennel bulb, which also contains the anti-spasmodic oils, can be used in soups or stews.

Lavender (*Lavandula officinalis*)

Lavender is balancing and soothing, having a sedative effect on the central nervous system and releasing muscle tension. When it comes to getting to sleep, lavender beats counting sheep. In one small 1995 study, researchers found that infusing the scent of lavender into the rooms of nursing home patients worked just as effectively as sleep medication.

If you recreate the natural conditions of this Mediterranean plant, it will be happiest. It likes sun and a dry, rocky soil that forces it to struggle slightly. When young, however, lavender is thirsty so water it in well. Never allow its roots to get soggy, especially in winter.

To aid sleep, make lavender into small sachets that can be slipped between your pillows. When the flowers open, cut the stalks, tie in small bunches and leave to dry out of direct sunlight – this will take two to four weeks, depending on the humidity levels.

Lavender also makes an unusual aromatic tea: add one teaspoon dried or two teaspoons of fresh blossoms to a cup of boiling water and steep for 10 minutes. Drink just before bedtime to nudge you sleep-wards. Lavender essential oil is very good for burns, and is one of the only essential oils that can be applied neat to skin safely.

Marigold (*Calendula officinalis*)

The bold orange petals of the marigold are valued highly for their anti-inflammatory powers and are used externally for healing wounds and skin irritations. An infused oil can easily be made at home. Just heat 100 g (3½ oz) dried marigold flowers in 500 ml (18 fl oz) olive or sunflower oil in a double boiler (or bain marie) for around three hours. Be sure to keep the water in the lower pan topped up to ensure that it does not boil dry. After this time, it will take on a golden colour and can then be strained and squeezed through a muslin cloth (or some kitchen paper). Keep the oil in a screw-top jar, and use it to moisturize dry skin, or swish some into the bath water to ease the symptoms of eczema.

Milk thistle (*Silybum marianum*)

The seeds of the milk thistle, whose spiky leaves look as though they have been splashed with milk, are one of the best-known herbal remedies for supporting the detoxifying process of the liver. Thus milk thistle is an ideal cure for hangovers – or it can be taken as a preventive measure.

This stunningly architectural plant grows to almost 2 m (6 ft) in height, and it is most content in a sunny, well-drained position. Harvest when the purple, almost artichoke-like flowers have matured into seed heads. You will need to wear gloves as they are very prickly. Place the seed heads in a warm, dry place inside a paper bag, and, after a few days, shake the heads to release the seeds. Prepare as a decoction (see page 186).

Passiflora *(Passiflora incarnata)*

Passion flower is a very gentle but effective sedative and painkiller which also brings down blood pressure. Take note of this if your blood pressure is already low. You will find it in a wide range of over-the-counter products for anxiety and nervous conditions (it is often blended with hops and/or valerian). It can also be enjoyed as a home-grown infusion.

A beautiful climber with exotic purple flowers, it can grow or spread to 6 m (18 ft). It thrives in fertile, well-drained soil and prefers partial shade. Passion flower can also be grown in a pot, although it will not reach such impressive heights.

The leaves and flowers can be harvested in summer and prepared as an infusion: put a teaspoon of the dried leaves in a mug, cover with water and drink after you have allowed it to steep for 10 minutes or so. This infusion is not only calming to the nerves but also can be helpful for period pains or tension headaches, and some people have found it beneficial in treating other nervous conditions, such as irritable bowel syndrome.

Sage *(Salvia officinalis)*

This is one of the best remedies for a sore mouth, throat or tonsils. Traditionally, it has also been associated with longevity; one old country rhyme tells us that '…he who drinks sage in May shall live for aye'. Certainly, sage contains powerful antioxidants and it is also rich in oestrogen; herbalists often prescribe sage tea, drunk regularly, to help ease some of the symptoms of the menopause.

There are many different types of sage but herbalists tend to prefer the purple variety (*Salvia officinalis* of the Purpurascens group). It can grow up to 1 m (3 ft) in height, if you give it ideal conditions. It should be harvested before flowering and then dried and prepared as an infusion (see page 186) for use as a tea, gargle or mouthwash.

Spearmint *(Mentha spicata)*

Spearmint, which is also sometimes referred to as common mint or garden mint, is best known as a stomach soother, aiding digestion while easing stomach spasms. It is also warming and a decongestant if you have got a cold or catarrh.

However, anyone who has ever sipped a steamy cup of spearmint tea will also be aware of the mood-lift that it can deliver, as spearmint contains a number of central nervous system stimulants, including menthol, which boost energy more gently than caffeine. Several of those stimulants are thought to sharpen our mental energy by preserving a neurotransmitter which is vital to memory and learning. The mint also boosts blood flow.

Spearmint can be raised from seed, but it is easier to grow from a small plant – or one that has been divided from a friend's plant. However, beware! Once planted, it can make a takeover bid in your herb garden and the new shoots will pop up everywhere, so it is sometimes the best thing to restrict its growth by planting it in a pot. Spearmint will thrive even in partial shade, but it will flourish best in some damp, cool soil.

Rosemary *(Rosmarinus officinalis)*

Simply crush a sprig of rosemary in your hands and it will help to sharpen your memory or boost concentration, as the scent stimulates blood flow to the brain. It is a circulatory stimulant which also works on headaches, and is reported to ease depression in some people.

Like lavender, rosemary is a sun-loving plant which needs good drainage, so if you live in a cold place and are growing it in a pot, then bring it inside for the winter. Rosemary should be given a haircut at the end of the summer to stop it getting too leggy, but do not cut into any old wood as it will not regenerate.

Ancient scholars used to wear rosemary around their heads, but you do not have to go that far. Simply brew rosemary as a tea to be sipped whenever you are doing brain work. Just add one to two teaspoons of rosemary needles to one cup of boiling water, set aside to steep for five minutes, then add a squirt of lime juice (optional) and enjoy.

The essential oils of rosemary have also been found to be invaluable for easing the pain of arthritis and rheumatism, or general muscular aches. To make a simple herbal remedy, you just use 10 drops of rosemary essential oil to a teaspoon of sweet almond oil and then massage gently into the affected area. You can also add a few drops of rosemary essential oil or a rosemary infusion (see right) to the final rinse after shampooing. This will help to clear up dandruff and also enhance your hair shine.

Processing herbs

Infusions

Infusions can be made from most leafy herbs and flowers. They are basically teas, which are made by steeping a herb in some freshly-boiled water for about 10 minutes in a ceramic or glass teapot. Traditionally, 25 g (1 oz) of the herb chosen was used to 500 ml (18 fl oz) of water, which is enough for three doses. Allow the water to go just off the boil before you pour it over the plant, or some of the aromatic plant elements will be lost in the steam. Strain before use. You can sweeten an infusion to taste with some honey, if you like.

Decoctions

Like infusions, decoctions are 'teas', but they are brewed from tougher plant components – bark, roots and berries, for instance – where it can be more difficult to extract the active elements.

- You should use 25 g (1 oz) plant material to 900 ml (1½ pints) cold water and bring to the boil in a glass, ceramic or stainless steel saucepan (do not use an aluminium pan).
- Allow to simmer gently until the liquid has reduced by around one-third and then strain out the plant material; you will have enough for three doses.
- You may want to warm up the decoction before drinking it; add some honey to taste if you have a sweet tooth.
- Leftover decoctions can be kept in the fridge for up to 48 hours.

The green home

We all want to live comfortably. We want our homes to delight our senses and nurture our soul, as well as providing heat, light and a space to retreat to and call our own. But, at the same time, many of us would like to reduce the impact that our twenty-first century lifestyles make on the world's resources. It may not be possible to grow your own paint or fabric – or make your own solar panel – but it is possible to enjoy a greener, more organic way of living in our homes. It can even save money. The good news is that we can live comfortably and warmly and be both stylish and green, at the same time. Making some simple lifestyle shifts to 'green' your home should also be the first step towards a healthier life for you and your family.

Green cleaning

This is just one of the simple ways in which you can make a difference – and 'tread more lightly' on the planet. Check under the typical kitchen sink and you will find dozens of individual cleaning products, designed to do everything from cleaning the oven to polishing the floor.

Many of these everyday cleaning products are based on chlorine bleaches, which release harmful organo-chlorines into the environment – as well as causing skin irritation. Nobody is suggesting that you adopt the Quentin Crisp 'dust-doesn't-get-any-worse-after-the-first-four-years' approach to cleaning, but there are some natural 'green' alternatives to this formidable armoury of chemicals.

Happily, there are many effective 'green cleaners' on the market today (see page 205 for brands and manufacturers). These have been vastly improved since they first appeared in the late 1980s, and they are worth revisiting if you dismissed them in the past. However, you do not even have to buy effective natural cleaning materials. Every home should also have the following all-natural, cheap-and-easy ingredients in its cleaning 'arsenal'.

Bicarbonate of soda
(sodium bicarbonate)

A solution of 2 tablespoons sodium bicarbonate to 500 ml (18 fl oz) water makes an effective non-abrasive cleaner – and also an excellent deodorizing fridge cleaner.

For a blocked sink, you can pour a teacup of bicarb down the plughole and the same amount of vinegar. Let it stand and fizz for about 10 minutes, and then pour boiling water slowly down the sink.

One of the most unpleasant household chemicals to use is oven cleaner. So next time you need to clean your oven, instead of using a caustic soda-based product, try rubbing the inside with a damp cloth which has been dipped in bicarbonate of soda immediately after using the oven – while it is still hot. Do take care not to burn yourself. When the oven has cooled down, leave for half-an-hour, then wipe clean.

Vinegar

Instead of window-cleaner, you could try using 2–5 tablespoons of white vinegar in 2 cups of water. Apply with a pump sprayer and then wipe off with an absorbent cloth.

Once a day, pour an eggcupful of vinegar down the lavatory, and then brush and flush; this is extremely effective and better for the environment than constantly flushing chemicals into the sewage system.

If it is used full strength, vinegar can make a great disinfectant for kitchen chopping boards and for bathroom fixtures. Used in the ratio 50:50 with water, any kind of vinegar (except balsamic!) also makes a brilliant glass cleaner or mirror cleaner. Cider vinegar is an excellent alternative to fabric softener – just a capful is enough to produce softness in your laundry when it is added to the washing machine during the final 'rinse' cycle.

Tea tree oil

Use 5 drops of an antiseptic oil, such as tea tree (or lavender or bergamot essential oil), in 1 litre (1.8 pints) water to wipe over kitchen surfaces, as a 'green' alternative to disinfectant. This will take a little more elbow grease, but it will give great results. Tea tree oil is also a magic mould-buster. Try adding two teaspoons of tea tree oil to 500 ml (18 fl oz) water, and then spritz onto shower curtains, where the roof has leaked – and anywhere else that's musty or mouldy. Do not rinse.

> ## More alternatives…
>
> ● Instead of using air freshener, you can add 25 drops of grapefruit oil to a plant-mister full of water, then shake well and use to dispel tobacco smoke or stale smells. Aerosol air fresheners, which are used by 41 per cent of householders, are linked with ear infections in children, headaches and even post-natal depression, according to a study by researchers at Bristol University.
>
> ● Preserve pine furniture by polishing with 5 drops of pine essential oil in 50 ml (2 fl oz) of sweet almond oil, which will disguise any early signs of age; allow to soak in and then buff to a shine.
>
> ● Moth balls contain particularly unpleasant chemicals: when storing clothes, use citronella, lavender or lemon on pieces of cotton wool, dotted around your clothing drawer to repel moths. Alternatively, invest in cedar blocks which are naturally repellent to insects; they may need gentle rubbing down every year or so with sandpaper, to release more of the cedar scent that moths hate.
>
> ● Roll a little new white bread into a ball and use it as an eraser for grubby marks on wallpaper and non-washable wall finishes.
>
> ● For lime scale on plug holes, rub with a cut lemon.
>
> ● Traditionally, strings of garlic, bundles of chilli peppers and pots of sage, thyme, oregano and basil were hung up in kitchens to ward off flies and other insects.

Greener machines

Unless we are being paid to do so for a step-back-in-time reality television history show, few of us want to return to the bad old days of scrubbing washing clean on a washboard, beating carpets with a brush or preparing supper over a campfire. Machines are now part of our lives.

There is absolutely no point in going out to buy a new, more energy-efficient machine just to replace the electricity-guzzling fridge you bought last time round. Replace appliances as they wear out – and ensure that when you do have to make this kind of investment, that you buy the most energy-efficient appliance that fits your needs. This is much easier now that everything from fridges to electric ovens has to have an energy rating symbol displayed – 'A' being the most energy-efficient, 'B' the next-best-thing, etc.

The next time that you are out shopping for a big electrical appliance for your home, don't just bear in mind how it is going to look in your kitchen or its energy rating but also consider the following factors.

Fridges and freezers

Make sure that your fridge/freezer is the right size for your needs – and your family's. A large fridge which has the same energy rating as a smaller fridge still uses more energy – and it generates more greenhouse gas emissions. If you have two fridges (many homes do), switch off the second fridge unless you need it for a special event. There is no point using energy to cool a near-empty fridge. Locate your fridge in a cool spot with good air circulation – it will not have to work so hard to keep everything chilled. Keep the door seals clean, and set the temperature as low as possible.

Cookers

Gas cooking is far more energy-efficient than using an electric cooker, saving up to half a tonne of greenhouse gas a year. If you do cook with electricity, for maximum efficiency you should use pots and pans that perfectly match the size of the element. Even simple actions, such as keeping the lid on while cooking, can reduce energy use.

Dishwashers

Electric dishwashers can generate hundreds of pounds of greenhouse gas each year. If you need one, choose the most energy-efficient model, but remember: the greenest energy for dishwashing is your own!

Microwave ovens

Although microwaves are highly energy efficient – using just a short blast of energy to heat up food – there are question marks over the safety of microwave use, according to some experts. The Environment Health Trust reports that cooking or heating our food in microwave ovens may cause molecular damage which, when eaten, may lead to abnormal changes in human blood, with a possible negative impact on the immune system. In a small but well-controlled trial, eight people were given either microwaved or normally cooked food over a few days. Blood samples were taken before and at intervals after the meals. Although the blood samples of those people eating normally-cooked food showed little change, the blood of those who had eaten microwaved food showed a drop in the white blood cells that are vital to immune system activity. Nobody knows whether this will have any long-term effects, but, if it does concern you, you should keep microwave use to an absolute minimum.

Meanwhile, to keep energy use for cooking as low as possible, why not consider making wholesome raw or lightly stir-fried dishes a bigger part of your diet – which is, of course, another great way for you to enjoy the 'taste dividend' of fresh, organic foods.

Washing machines

Laundries are high water and energy users – so there is plenty of scope for savings here. Choose an energy-efficient machine which is right for the size of your household – a machine that is too large will often be used when it is half-full, gobbling up extra energy.

Use water as cool as is effective to get your clothes clean – experiment and you may be surprised at the results. And remember that using more detergent than the recommended 'dose' does not get the clothes cleaner! If you halve or even quarter the amount of powder that you put in your washing and dishwashing machines, the chances are that the wash will come out just as clean.

Tumble driers

In a perfect (non-rainy) world, we would not use these at all. A tumble drier generates more than 3 kg (7 lb) of greenhouse gas for each load you dry. Compare that with a washing line – which uses no energy at all (except a bit of yours, pegging your wash out to dry).

Greener, cleaner power

If possible, you could sign up for one of the new 'green power' services. These enable you to buy your power from renewable sources, usually wind power, but potentially solar and wave power, in the future, as these energy technologies start feeding into the national grid. It is a simple matter of filling in a form and changing your supplier – and then the power company takes care of the rest.

Why is 'green' power so important? Because by buying power from conventional suppliers, we are contributing to greenhouse gas emissions generated at coal-fired power stations – which, in turn, may be encouraging global warming.

So although green power may in some instances be costing your household just a little more, you can feel comfortable in the knowledge that your small step is also driving investment in renewable energy projects – and helping to slow the warming of the globe.

Saving energy

We can save energy – and our household bills – in a variety of different ways, whether it's keeping an eye on the electricity we use and switching off lights or switching off the television when it's not in use.

Light

Where would we be without electric light? Simple: in the dark. However, while lighting is essential in our homes and workspaces, there are simple steps we can take to make sure we miminize the environmental impact of living 'illuminated' twenty-first century lives.

Getting in the habit of switching off lights in rooms that are not being used is a major step towards saving energy (albeit one that teenagers, in particular, have trouble grasping). Buying energy-efficient light bulbs is another. Traditional light bulbs use 90 per cent of their energy emitting heat – not light – which just goes to show how wasteful they are, in energy terms. Modern light bulbs use up to 70 per cent less electricity than traditional types, last more than 10 times longer (typically, with a lifespan of 10,000 hours) and emit far less heat. Although they require an initial investment and are more expensive than conventional bulbs, they do save money over their lifetime – by reducing your electricity bill.

Meanwhile, if you are thinking of lighting your garden – and be aware that it can interfere with birds' body clocks – then you should opt for one of the many types of solar-powered light, which store up the sun's energy by day and then release it after dark.

Electromagnetic fields

These invisible forces are produced by electricity and emitted by electrical appliances. Some experts think they have possible links to health problems, like brain tumours and breast cancer. To protect yourself, keep TVs, electric clocks and other appliances at least 1 m (3 ft) away from where you are sitting or sleeping; after that distance, EMFs drop off rapidly. Electric blankets are potentially very dangerous if you sleep with them on, as they stay plugged in (and hot) and lie directly over or under your body for hours, exposing you to a stream of EMFs all night long. Switch to a hot water bottle or at least turn off the blanket while you sleep.

Energy dilemmas

Most of us want a more energy-efficient home but also to strike a balance between energy efficiency and good health. Modern homes, with double glazing, draught-excluding strips on windows and no chimneys, don't allow air to circulate so efficiently. Only you can decide which is more important: fresher air, which may lead to fewer allergies or even asthma, or greater energy savings. This is one of the 'green dilemmas' that faces us in our century – but it helps to be armed with all the relevant information

Water, water everywhere…

We all take running water so much for granted that it is easy to think it is endless, but, in reality, water is a precious and limited resource. A leaking lavatory can waste thousands of litres a month. A dripping tap might waste up to nine litres a minute! But there are all sorts of things we do without even thinking of the water we waste. Here are some simple guidelines to help you use it more wisely.

● Always wait until you have a full load of washing or dishes for the dishwasher.
● Never wash dishes under a running tap; fill a basin, instead, and do a few at a time.
● Always use a bucket rather than a hose to wash the car.
● Remember that plants love 'waste' water, also known as 'grey' water, which has already been used for cooking and washing.
● Collect the rainwater we all tend to let go – consider a water butt, even in a city. You can now buy 'half-butts', which take up 50 per cent of the space and are perfect even for tiny roof decks or yards.
● Taking shorter showers will save water – and energy, too. In fact, up to 40 per cent of home energy costs come from water heating – much of that for baths and showers. If you keep it short – especially if you fit an efficient shower-head and, better still, a water aerator, less energy will be needed to heat your water, which will cut the cost of your heating bill.

Recycle, recycle, recycle

Sometimes this is easier said than done as many local authorities still offer appallingly restricted recycling facilities, and some householders find it literally impossible to find a way of recycling cardboard and many plastics. However, most waste starts in the kitchen, so set up a system that makes it easy and convenient to separate your paper and cardboard (if you're lucky enough to be able to recycle that) from tins, glass, plastic and organic matter – which can be turned into compost. There are really good reasons for composting: when food and garden waste are buried in landfill, they break down to form a mixture of gases, including methane, a potent greenhouse gas. Three or four times as much of those gases is produced in landfill than if that organic waste is allowed to break down naturally in the presence of air – in a compost heap or a wormery.

If you do not have outside space – because you live in a flat, perhaps – then you may not have much choice. However, even the tiniest balcony can accommodate a wormery – and you can than use the rich compost that it produces to grow your own vegetables, such as tomatoes, in pots or organic grow bags. How's that for a virtuous circle?

Don't just think about recycling

Think about not creating waste in the first place. Packaging creates mountains of unnecessary rubbish. Look for products that are packaged in recyclable materials. Always buy refills and carry your own bag or basket – calico or mesh bags fit easily in your handbag. Just do it.

Clear the air

You are probably concerned about pollution outside – just cross the road and smell that horrible carbon monoxide. But, in reality, the air quality inside our homes often leaves a lot to be desired, too.

A study into indoor air pollution carried out by the UK government's Building Research Establishment has revealed that pollution may be 10 times worse inside the home than outside it, and that the quality of the air we breathe at home poses a greater risk to health than breathing city smog.

So who are the culprits? American research into indoor pollution has measured significant amounts of chloroform – a toxic gas released when chlorinated water turns to steam in hot showers – in indoor environments. They also detected high levels of tetrachloroethylene – dry-cleaning fluid (which has been shown to cause cancer in laboratory animals) – from clothes which were hung in the wardrobe, fresh from the cleaners, without being aired

first. Add to that the battery of cleaning materials and fluids that we use on a daily basis to keep our homes spick and span, and you begin to get an idea of how our bodies, and minds, are constantly assaulted by chemicals which our systems have not evolved to cope with. In the United States, the Environmental Protection Agency estimates that up to 6,000 cancer deaths annually are brought about by indoor air pollutants. And as Michael McIntyre, Head of the School of Chinese Herbal Medicine, points out: 'Right now, we're carrying out the biggest chemical experiment in history on ourselves.'

However, in spite of all this doom and gloom, happily, there is plenty we can all do to reduce our exposure to the chemicals around us.

A healthier home

Here are some simple steps and guidelines that you can follow to create a healthier environment in your own home:

● Do make sure you get your central heating serviced every year.

● Don't seal any room in your house where there is a fuel-burning appliance; fresh air is swiftly used up, while irritating gases and excessive carbon monoxide build up.

● Do check that your ventilation is good and that the flues are not blocked. Ensure that there is a permanent vent in any room which has a gas appliance.

● Don't let stale air build up in the house; open the windows and doors regularly at the back and front of the building to encourage 'through' ventilation.

● Do use water-based paints and keep the windows open while you are doing any kind of decorating in your home.

● Do increase humidity if the air is dry. Try a ceramic aromatherapy burner; add an essential oil to water and then heat with a night-light; this not only creates moisture but also delivers soothing scents.

● Do consider rugs on wooden floors instead of wall-to-wall carpet. As Michael McIntyre, Head of the School of Chinese Herbal Medicine in the UK, points out: 'Our parents had rugs, which were regularly beaten. And incidences of breathing problems and allergies, for instance, were much, much lower in those days.'

● Do use beeswax and linseed oil in place of spritz-on furniture polishes – and generally get into the habit of using only natural products and pump-action sprays.

● Don't buy vinyl flooring; linoleum and wood are less toxic choices.

● Do get any old pipes replaced; lead pipes can poison the water.

● Don't put dry-cleaned clothes away in the wardrobe immediately; remove the plastic wrapping and air them by an open window before you store them. Taking a little time to air your clothes, and brushing them clean, is a great way to avoid excessive dry cleaning, which also knocks the stuffing out of clothes.

● Do wear two pairs of gloves whenever you are using household chemicals, paints and varnishes. You need a thin disposable plastic or rubber pair (like surgeons wear) underneath durable rubber gloves. 'Many of the chemicals that you buy in a do-it-yourself store are the same as those used in industry, where health and safety regulations make it compulsory to wear protective gloves,' explains Michael McIntyre. 'The skin is extremely porous so it's easy for those chemicals to enter the bloodstream via contact.'

● Do avoid foam fillings for mattresses and furniture next time you replace the current ones; futons and cotton mattresses are the healthiest options.

● Don't get furniture, carpets or curtains stain-proofed, as this is a highly chemical process. If you're really worried about stains, think about colours that will not show the dirt, instead – or are easily washable.

● Do test paints before you paint a whole room with them, to establish any sensitivity. There is no such thing as completely non-toxic paint, but some are less toxic than others (see right). According to John Bower, director of the Healthy House Institute in Bloomington, Indiana, 'Although it airs out eventually, some people have been known to be bothered by paint that's a year old.' Most natural paint companies will, for a small charge, supply product samples that can be used for testing. These come in small 'tester' pots, which also help you decide whether a colour is right for your décor as well as alerting you to whether the smell lingers. Enlist the help of your builder in your quest for healthier building materials. Most builders' merchants and even D-I-Y shops are becoming more aware of the potential risks from building materials, solvents and paints and can steer you towards the least harmful options, if you ask questions.

In addition, drink mint tea whenever you have used paint, varnishes or any other toxic chemicals. Mint tea can help the body to eliminate toxins like these or indeed those created by any similar procedure (e.g. staining wood floors) from the system more quickly.

'Green' paints

With the vast choice of natural paints that are available today, you can decorate your home with any colour of the rainbow – and still be 'green'. Decorative paints are a major source of atmospheric pollution and they are also implicated in Sick Building Syndrome, giving off dangerous fumes, including benzene and toluene, as well as fungicides.

One hundred million litres of hydrocarbon and related solvents are said to be released into the atmosphere every year by the UK paint industry – greenhouse gases that may be contributing to global warming. By contrast, 'greener' paints are made from natural pigments and oils but still deliver the finishes, shade range and effects that even the most design-conscious home-lover could wish for. The key is to look for the words 'low-VOC', 'VOC-free' or 'low biocide' on the label. For more information, turn to page 205.

Houseplants for health

The good news for all you plant-lovers is that the humble houseplant is emerging as the greatest weapon against less-than-fresh air. It seems, in fact, that it is even possible to grow fresh air.

In the 1960s, NASA (the National Aeronautics and Space Administration) was faced with the challenge of creating a life-support system for planned moon bases. They began studies on treating and recycling air and waste water, which led to scientists asking the important question: how does the Earth sustain and produce clean air? The answer, of course, was through the living cycle of plants, which led to the discovery that houseplants – from rubber plants to palms, ferns and figs – could revitalize and purify air in sealed test chambers. How does this work? Plants clean the air by absorbing toxins which provide nutrients for micro organisms around the plants' roots, where they are broken down into harmless sugars and good old oxygen. In an ideal world, we would turn our homes into a veritable mini-jungle, but in the quest for fresher indoor air, some plants are more efficient than others.

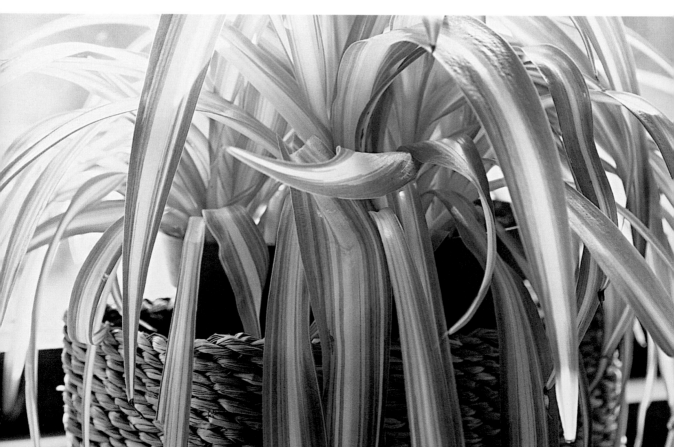

Basic guide to healthy house plants

Name	What it does	Positioning	Care
Areca palm (*Chrysalidocarpus lutescens*)	One of the best houseplants tested for chasing away chemical toxins, including xylene and formaldehyde, while releasing large amounts of moisture into the air. (Winter colds and allergy attacks are often aggravated by low indoor humidity.)	This is best for reception areas because of its size; it can grow up to 5 m (15 ft) high.	It grows well in filtered sunlight; it needs year-round warmth and ample humidity so it should be misted regularly, both to freshen it up and discourage insects.
Boston Fern (*Nephrolepis exaltata bostoniensis*)	Of all the plants tested, this one scored the highest for removing air pollutants (especially formaldehyde) and retaining moisture.	Put one or two of these ferns in a room where there is new carpeting or furniture.	Easy to grow in medium to bright light; water when the soil feels dry and mist regularly to keep leaves from turning brown and dropping.
English ivy (*Hedera helix*)	In tests in a sealed chamber, English ivy removed 90 per cent of the benzene; it's also effective at removing formaldehyde and xylene (a colourless liquid which comes from petroleum, and which is found in many building materials).	This is especially effective in any room that has been freshly painted or carpeted. It is also good in a room that contains plastic equipment or furnishings (computers, fax machines, printers, etc.) or ink.	This is easy to grow in bright light; mist often, especially when the air is quite dry.
Peace lily (*Spathiphyllum sp.*)	The peace lily excels in removing alcohols, acetone, trichlorethylene, formaldehyde and benzene from indoor air.	Good anywhere, particularly near office equipment. Also, think about keeping one near your wardrobe, to soak up any vapours from dry cleaning fluids.	Feed regularly from spring to autumn; keep the soil evenly moist during the growing season and slightly drier during the winter. Wipe the leaves occasionally to remove insect attack.
Spider plant (*Chlorophytum comosum*)	In tests in a sealed chamber, spider plants removed 96 per cent of the potentially deadly gas carbon monoxide; also good for removing xylene and formaldehyde.	Useful in kitchens with gas stoves or any rooms with fireplaces.	Easy to grow in bright to medium light; rotate regularly to ensure even growth. Feed in spring and summer.
Striped dracaena 'Janet Craig' (*Draceaena deremensis* 'Janet Craig')	What it does: Much valued as an office plant for its ability to soak up trichlorethylene, a chemical released by photocopiers and printers.	Near your home computer or on a kitchen windowsill; its near-relative, *Dracaena compacta*, can tolerate neglect and dimly-lit rooms so is good for areas where other plants would give up the ghost and die.	Almost indestructible and can live for decades; does best in semi-shade. Keep the soil moist but not soggy and repot once every two years.

Natural furnishings

Living the organic life isn't just about health, beauty and wellbeing. There is now a wide range of natural fabrics, furniture and floorings that can help to create a soothing, stylish interior in your home.

Natural floorings

If you look in any glossy homes magazine, you will see that natural floorings, such as sisal, jute and coir, have become really fashionable. These natural fibre floorings come from various renewable crops, such as grasses and coconuts, and they are now widely available in a choice of patterns, which range from checks to herringbone.

However, there are several ways of laying them, some of which are healthier than others. Some natural flooring companies recommend sticking down the flooring using a potent-smelling glue, the fumes from which can linger in the home for quite some time. From an environmental point of view, you may choose instead to have the flooring 'stapled' – the staples are all but invisible. You can discuss this with your carpet fitter.

● Natural fibre floorings can stain, pick up dirt quite easily and be hard to clean. (Wet cleaning is not advisable as this flooring can shrink.) Manufacturers often recommend that they are treated with a stain-proofing treatment, which once again releases chemicals into the air for you and your family to breathe. If that does not appeal, consider a 'no-shoe' policy indoors, or keep your natural flooring to areas that are low-traffic, like bedrooms. Your home will become much cleaner, as a bonus, without dirt being tramped all over it from the outside world.

● Wooden flooring is another natural choice, but always check that the material comes from managed forests. You might also like to look for the Soil Association's 'woodmark', which communicates that the wood has come from an organic wood or forest. Salvage yards can also be a treasure trove of reclaimed wooden flooring – from boards to intricate parquets.

● Tiles are another 'green' choice; they look gorgeous (as do wooden floors) when strewn with rugs. Reclaimed terracotta tiles can also be found in salvage yards.

● Linoleum is also worth your consideration. Good old 'lino', now marketed as Marmoleum, is a hessian-backed linoleum which is made from natural resins and is available in a wide range of incredibly durable colours. Vinyl flooring, by contrast, is made from the plastic PVC and may represent a hazard to children, as it can contain phthalates – known to have damaging effects on the body's hormones.

Organic fabrics

The Soil Association has textile standards so you can look for their symbol on sustainable fabrics – which can, of course, be used for curtains, cushions, upholstery and bedding.

Sleep sweetly

We spend one-third of our lives in bed – so the quality of our sheets really matters. Next time you need to buy some new sheets, make sure that you shop for organic cotton.

The fibres in conventionally produced sheets and blankets, especially if they have a 'no-iron' finish, can be laden with chemicals like formaldehyde (which is used to control shrinking), fire-retardants, dyes and other ingredients which release VOCs (Volatile Organic Compounds, or basically, toxic gases) into the atmosphere.

If you are not sure that you want to snuggle up with all those chemicals, then take the extra trouble to look for organic cotton, rather than sheets which just claim to be 'natural' cotton. The claim that cotton is 'natural' or 'green' probably means that it has not been dyed with chemicals or 'finished' with other toxic substances – but it may well still have come from conventional (non-organic) agriculture, or contain GM cotton.

Cotton is the world's most heavily-sprayed field crop. Planted on only around three per cent of arable land, it accounts for 25 per cent of the total pesticides and herbicides used annually in the world. Or, put another way, it takes more than half a kilo of agricultural chemicals to produce a set of sheets for a double bed. What's more, the pesticides and herbicides used to grow many fibres do not readily break down in water, so they can stay on bed linen even after the material has been washed several times. That won't kill anyone, but do you really want to sleep cocooned by chemicals? Organic cotton, by contrast, is grown entirely naturally – and many people who sleep in it have nothing but praise for its softness on the skin.

Meanwhile, when you next have to replace your mattress, buy a natural fibre version made from horse hair, coconut fibre, wool or even straw. Experts recommend that for optimum health and sleep comfort, our mattresses should be replaced every 10 years.

Sofa, so good...

Most new furniture, carpeting and upholstery contains formaldehyde as well as toxic resins and adhesives. However, there are some healthier alternatives. For instance, do not be so quick to dump the old in favour of the brand, spanking new. Here are some practical suggestions that you can consider.

● Get the same purchasing kick from buying secondhand – and saving some landfill space.

● Think about creating slipcovers from an environmentally-friendly fabric, such as hemp or organic cotton; try to find a good, friendly local upholsterer who can help you rediscover the beauty in a battered sofa or sagging chair.

● Think about the life cycle of your furniture before you buy it – and try not to buy what cannot be refurbished, resold or reused.

Shopping for furniture at antique (and junk) shops is one way to be sure that you are not contributing to the destruction of forests, and if you shop wisely (without slavishly following the latest interiors trend), you will be able to acquire heirlooms that can be handed down from generation to generation.

Appendix
Bibliography

A Colour Handbook of Biological Control in Plant Protection, Neil Helyer (Manson Publishing)

Artificial Incubation, Dr. Batty (Beech Publications)

Cobbett's Country Book (David and Charles)

Composting for All, Nicky Scott (Green Books)

Diseases of Free Range Poultry, Victoria Roberts (Whittet Books)

Diseases of Organic Vegetables, Peter Gladders (ADAS)

Domestic Ducks and Geese, Fred Hams (Shire Publications)

Ducks and Geese at Home, M. & V. Roberts (Golden Cockerel)

Grow Your Own Vegetables, Joy Larkcom (Frances Lincoln)

Growing Under Glass Without Using Chemicals, Sue Stickland (HDRA/Search Press)

Homeopathic Treatment for Birds, Beryl Chapman (C.W. Daniel Co. Ltd.)

Homoeopathy in Veterinary Practice, K.J. Biddis (C.W. Daniel Co. Ltd.)

Homoeopathy, The Shepherd's Guide, Mark Elliott and Tony Pinkus (Ainsworth's Homoeopathic Pharmacy)

Keeping a Few Ducks in Your Garden, Francine Raymond (The Kitchen Garden)

Keeping a Few Hens in Your Garden, Francine Raymond (The Kitchen Garden)

Knowing and Recognising, the Biology of Glasshouse Pests and Their Natural Enemies, M. H. Malais and W. J. Ravensberg Koppert (B. V. and Reed Business Information)

New Book of Herbs, Jekka McVicar (Dorling Kidersley)

Not On The Label – What Really Goes In The Food On Your Plate, Felicity Lawrence (Penguin)

Organic Vegetable Handbook, (NIAB)

Pests, Diseases & Disorders of Garden Plants, Stefan Buczacki and Keith Harris (HarperCollins)

Poultry House Construction, Michael Roberts (Gold Cockerel Books)

Poultry Houses and Appliances, Dr Batty (Beech Publishing)

Rotations for Organic Horticultural Field Crops, (Soil Association)

Seed to Seed, Suzanne Ashworth (Seed Saver Publications)

Seeds of Deception – Exposing Corporate and Government Lies about the Safety of Genetically Engineered Food, Jeffrey M. Smith (Green Books)

Shopped – The Shocking Power of British Supermarkets, Joanna Blythman (Fourth Estate)

So Shall We Reap – What's Gone Wrong With The World's Food – And How To Fix It, Colin Tudge (Penguin)

Soil Management on Organic Farms, Lois Phillips (Soil Association)

The Big Book of Garden Hens, Francine Raymond (The Kitchen Garden)

The British Poultry Club Standards (Blackwell Science)

The Complete Guide to Self-Sufficiency, John Seymour (Faber)

The Complete Herbal for Farm and Stable, J. de Bairacli Levy (Faber)

The Complete Know and Grow Vegetables, J. K. Bleasdale (Oxford University Press)

The Henry Doubleday Association Encyclopedia of Organic Gardening, Pauline Pears (editor-in-chief) (Dorling Kindersley)

The Herdsman's Introduction to Homoeopathy, Philip Hansford and Tony Pinkus (Ainsworth's Homoeopathic Pharmacy)

The New Seed-Starters Handbook, Nancy Bubel (Rodale Press)

The New Shopper's Guide to Organic Food, Lynda Brown (Fourth Estate)

The Organic Directory (Soil Association) 40–56 Victoria Street, Bristol BS1 6BY website: www.theorganicdirectory.co.uk

The Organic Salad Garden, Joy Larkcom (Frances Lincoln)

The Royal Horticultural Society Organic Gardening, Pauline Pears and Sue Stickland (Mitchell Beazley)

The Royal Horticultural Society New Encyclopedia of Herbs & their Uses, Deni Bown, (Dorling Kindersley)

The Treatment of Cattle by Homoeopathy, George McLeod (The Health Science Press)

The Veterinary Book for Sheep Farmers, David C. Henderson (Farming Press)

The Origins of the Organic Movement, Philip Conford (Floris Books)

Useful information

Grow your own

The Association For Organics Recycling
3 Burystead Place,
Wellingborough,
Northamptonshire, NN8 1AH
tel: 0870 160 3278
web: www.compost.org.uk

Brogdale Horticultural Trust
Brogdale Road, Faversham,
Kent ME13 8YZ
tel: 01795 535286
email: info@brogdale.org
web: www.brogdale.org.uk

Cats Protection
National Cat Centre,
Chelwood Gate,
Haywards Heath,
Sussex RH17 7TT
tel: 08702 099 099
email: helpline@cats.org.uk
web: www.cats.org.uk

Common Ground
Gold Hill House, 21 High Street,
Shaftesbury, Dorset SP7 8JE
tel: 01747 850820
www.commonground.org.uk

Garden Organic
Ryton-on-Dunsmore,
Coventry CV8 3LG
tel: 024 7630 3517
web: www.gardenorganic.org.uk
Will supply fact sheets on organic gardening, runs courses and produces a catalogue

Green Gardener
Brook Hill, Brundall Road,
Blofield NR13 4LB
tel: 01603 715096
email: jon@greengardener.co.uk
web: www.greengardener.co.uk

The Herb Society
Sulgrave Manor, Sulgrave,
Banbury, Oxfordshire X17 1XB
tel: 0845 4918699
web: www.herbsociety.co.uk

National Society of Allotment and Leisure Gardeners
O'Dell House, Hunters Road,
Corby NN17 5JE
tel: 01536 266576 (24 hour answerphone)
email: natsoc@nsalg.org.uk
web: www.nsalg.org.uk

Royal Society for the Protection of Birds (RSPB)
The Lodge, Sandy,
Bedfordshire SG19 2DL
tel: 01767 680551
web: www.rspb.org.uk

Home farm

Allen and Page (Organic GM Free Feed)
tel: 01362 822900

The British Call Duck Club
Maes y Coed, Llanarth,
Ceredigion SA47 0RG
tel: 01545 580425
www.britishcallduckclub.org.uk

British Cattle Movement Service
Curwen Road, Workington,
Cumbria CA14 2DD
tel: 0845 050 1234
email: ctsonline@bcms.rpa.gsi.gov.uk
web: www.bcms.gov.uk

British Pig Association
Trumpington Mews, 40b High
Street, Trumpington,
Cambridgeshire CB2 2LS
tel: 01223 845100
email: bpa@britishpigs.org
web: www.britishpigs.org

DEFRA
Customer Contact Unit, Eastbury
House, 30-34 Albert
Embankment, London SE1 7TL
tel: 08459 335577
email: helpline@defra.gsi.gov.uk
web: www.defra.gov.uk

The Domestic Fowl Trust
Station Road, Honeybourne,
Evesham WR11 7QZ
tel: 01386 833083
email: clive@domesticfowltrust.co.uk
web: www.domesticfowltrust.co.uk

The Domestic Waterfowl Club
Limetree Cottages,
Bright Walton, Newbury,
Berkshire RG20 7BZ
tel: 01488 638014
web: www.domestic-waterfowl.co.uk

Forsham Cottage Arks
tel: 01233 820229

Interhatch (incubator suppliers)
tel: 01246 264646

The Kitchen Garden
Troston, Suffolk IP31 1EX
tel: 01359 268322
www.kitchen-garden-hens.co.uk

Marriages (Organic Feed)
tel: 01245 354455

National Cattle Association
Tim Brigstocke, Brick House,
Risbury, Leominster,
Herefordshire HR6 0NQ
tel: 01568 760632
email: timbrigstocke@hotmail.com

Organic Farms Network
Soil Association, South Plaza,
Marlborough Street,
Bristol BS1 3NX
tel: 0117 314 5000
web: www.soilassociation.org

Oxford Bee Company Ltd
Ark Business Centre, Gordon
Road, Loughborough LE11 1JP
tel: 01509 261654
email: info@oxbeeco.com

The Poultry Club of Great Britain
Keepers Cottage,
40 Benvarden Road,
Dervock, Ballymoney,
Co. Antrim BT53 6NW
tel: 02820 741056
email: info@poultryclub.org
web: www.poultryclub.org

The organic home

Auro Organic Paints
website: www.auroorganic.co.uk

Ecos paints
web: www.ecospaints.com
Solvent free and odourless paints

Green Paints
website: www.greenshop.co.uk

Natural Collection
web: www.naturalcollection.com
Useful information on suitable green cleaning products

Nutshell (natural paints)
web: www.nutshellpaints.com

General

Organic Places to Stay (UK and Ireland)
by Linda Moss
tel: 01943 871468
web: www.organicholidays.com

The Soil Association

The Soil Association is a membership charity campaigning for planet friendly food and farming. It promotes the connection between soil, plants, animals, food, human health and the health of our planet.

The Soil Association relies on support from people like you. Please join the charity and help it speak out and influence positive change to the way food is produced. Your support helps to:

● Campaign on the issues you care about. From genetically modified crops and dangerous chemicals in food, to factory farming and the destruction of wildlife, your voice will be heard

● Build communities and connect people with how their food is produced

● Protect animal welfare

● Provide healthy, nutritious food in schools

● Create a sustainable and organic food and farming culture.

Benefits of membership

By joining the Soil Association you can help to build a better future for our planet. Your Soil Association membership includes:

● A welcome pack with guides to organic living and The Soil Association

● A membership card entitling you to hundreds of special offers and discounts at independent organic outlets, plus free entry to Soil Association organic festivals

● *Living Earth* – a quarterly magazine full of features, campaigning updates, reader offers and regular columns on organic cooking and gardening

● Invitations to special events such as farm walks, debates, lectures and master classes

● A wealth of information and a members only e-newsletter providing up to the minute information, hints and tips.
www.soilassociation.org/joinus

Visit an organic farm

The Soil Association has a network of organic farms which the public can visit. These farms often have open days, special events, farm trails and farm shops. For more information please visit: www.soilassociation.org/farmvisits

Producer Members

The Soil Association offers technical advice for anyone interested in organic techniques; whether you are a smallholder, researcher or farmer. For an annual fee you can become a Producer Member, which gives you access to technical guides, fact sheets, a telephone helpline and many hands-on training events.

Food for Life Partnership

The Soil Association led Food for Life Partnership aims to revolutionise school meals, reconnect young people with farms and inspire families to cook and grow food. Schools across England can join the Food for Life Partnership and win awards for transforming their food culture. www.foodforlife.org.uk

Genetic modification

For the latest news on genetic modification and the different ways to campaign, visit our website: www.soilassociation.org/gm

Organic Directory

The Organic Directory is your comprehensive UK guide to everything organic. You can find sources of organic food, farmers' markets, organic vegetable box schemes, places to stay, toiletries, beauty and cosmetic products, baby products, clothing, household products and much more. You can buy a copy of *The Organic Directory* (Green Books) or view it for free at: www.theorganicdirectory.co.uk

Eat Organic, Buy Local

The Soil Association has a department dedicated to supporting the development of local organic food. Working with farmers, growers and consumers they have been instrumental in the successful growth of box schemes and farmers markets and continue to promote new types of local food initiatives to create a popular and thriving food culture. Community Supported Agriculture is the most recent approach linking consumers even more closely with farmers. Farmers receive committed support through members providing a secure income whilst consumers receive fresh local produce and can get involved on the farm. For more information on Community Supported Agriculture visit: www.soilassociation.org/csa

Organic seeds

Five years ago, there were only 50 organic seed varieties available, but now farmers and growers can choose from almost 1,200. Working with the seed industry, the Soil Association has played a key role in making organic seed widely available. It also manages a website that is dedicated to organic seed – www.organicxseeds.com – where farmers and growers can source organic seed. For more information about organic seed call the food and farming department on 0117 914 2400 or email ff@soilassociation.org

Contact us

Soil Association

South Plaza, Marlborough Street,
Bristol BS1 3NX
tel: 0117 314 5000
email: info@soilassociation.org
website: www.soilassociation.org

Soil Association Scotland

Tower Mains, 18 Liberton Brae,
Edinburgh EH16 6EA
tel: 0131 666 2474
email: contact@soilassociation.org
website: www.soilassociationscotland.org

Organic Centre Wales

website: www.organic.aber.ac.uk